CW00537688

33

STUDY GUIDE

Russia, 1905 - 1941

CIE

app
available

Published by Clever Lili Limited.

contact@cleverlili.com

First published 2020

ISBN 978-1-913887-32-2

Cover by: Manipulated image by pict rider on Adobe Stock

Icons by: flaticon and freepik

Contributors: Lynn Harkin, Hayleigh Snow, Nicola Nicholls, Shahan Abu Shumel Haydar

Edited by Paul Connolly and Rebecca Parsley

Design by Evgeni Veskov and Will Fox

DISCOVER MORE OF OUR IGCSE HISTORY STUDY GUIDES

GCSEHistory.com and Clever Lili

STUDY GUIDE
International Relations:
Were the Peace Treaties of 1919-23 Fair?
GCSEHistory.com
17

CIE
STUDY GUIDE
International Relations:
To What Extent Was the League of Nations a Success?
GCSEHistory.com
18

CIE
STUDY GUIDE
International Relations:
Why Had International Peace Collapsed by 1939?
GCSEHistory.com
19

CIE
STUDY GUIDE
International Relations:
Who Was to Blame for the Cold War?
GCSEHistory.com
20

CIE
STUDY GUIDE
International Relations:
How Effectively Did the United States Contain the Spread of Communism?
GCSEHistory.com
21

CIE
STUDY GUIDE
International Relations:
How Secure Was the USSR's Control Over Eastern Europe, 1948 - 1989?
GCSEHistory.com
22

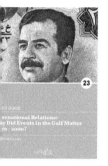

CIE
STUDY GUIDE
International Relations:
Why Did Events in the Gulf Matter 1970 - 2000?
GCSEHistory.com
23

CIE
STUDY GUIDE
The United States, 1919 - 1941
GCSEHistory.com
32

CIE
STUDY GUIDE
The First World War, 1914 - 1918
GCSEHistory.com
31

CIE
STUDY GUIDE
Germany, 1918 - 1945
GCSEHistory.com
34

CIE
STUDY GUIDE
China, c1950-1990
GCSEHistory.com
46

Contents

In this study guide, you will see a series of icons, highlighted words and page references. The key below will help you quickly establish what these mean and where to go for more information.

Icons

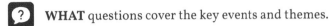 **WHAT** questions cover the key events and themes.

WHO questions cover the key people involved.

WHEN questions cover the timings of key events.

WHERE questions cover the locations of key moments.

WHY questions cover the reasons behind key events.

HOW questions take a closer look at the way in which events, situations and trends occur.

IMPORTANCE questions take a closer look at the significance of events, situations, and recurrent trends and themes.

DECISIONS questions take a closer look at choices made at events and situations during this era.

Highlighted words

Abdicate - occasionally, you will see certain words highlighted within an answer. This means that, if you need it, you'll find an explanation of the word or phrase in the glossary which starts on **page 128**.

Page references

Tudor *(p.7)* - occasionally, a certain subject within an answer is covered in more depth on a different page. If you'd like to learn more about it, you can go directly to the page indicated.

Russia, 1905-41 is the depth study that investigates why and how the tsarist regime collapsed in 1917 and was transformed into a communist dictatorship between 1917 and 1941. You will focus on the crucial events and people of this period, as well as studying the different social, cultural, political, economic, military and religious changes that occurred.

Purpose
This study will help you to understand the complexities of political change and control. You will investigate themes such as power, law and order, revolution, government, censorship, propaganda, art and culture, communism, dictatorship, economy and society. You will develop the skills of explaining, analysing and making judgements about events, beliefs, people and situations. You will use the concepts of cause, consequences, change, continuity, similarity, difference and significance to construct valid historical explanations.

Topics
Russia, 1905-41 is split into 4 key enquiries.

- Enquiry 1 looks at the reasons why Tsar Nicholas II's reign ended in 1917. You will investigate to how Tsar Nicholas survived the 1905 revolution, and to what extent he successfully dealt with the issues facing Russia up to 1914. You will study the impact of the First World War on Russia and why the revolution of March 1917 was successful.

- Enquiry 2 looks at how and why the Bolsheviks gained and consolidated power from 1917 to 1924. You will investigate the successes and failures of the Provisional Government after the March Revolution and why the Bolsheviks were successful in the November 1917 revolution. You will study how the Bolsheviks consolidated power in the Civil War and evaluate the impact of their New Economic Policy.

- Enquiry 3 looks at Stalin's rise to power and how he created a personal dictatorship. You will investigate how Stalin won the leadership struggle between 1924 and 1929, and the reasons behind the purges of the 1930s. You will explore how Stalin controlled the USSR, and to what extent that control was secure by 1941.

- Enquiry 4 looks at Stalin's economic policies and their impact on the USSR. You will study why the Five Year Plans and collectivisation were introduced and evaluate their impact. You will investigate the how far these policies transformed the lives of the peoples of the USSR.

Key Individuals
Some of the key individuals studied on this course include:

- Tsar Nicholas II.
- Tsarina Alexandra.
- Grigori Rasputin.
- Vladimir Lenin.
- Joseph Stalin.
- Leon Trotsky.
- Alexander Kerensky.
- Pyotr Stolypin.

Key Events
Some of the key events you will study on this course include:

- Bloody Sunday, 1905.
- The effect of the First World War on Russia.
- The February Revolution, 1917.
- The Russian Civil War.
- The consolidation of Bolshevik control.
- The New Economic Policy.
- The Five Year Plans.
- Stalin's cult of personality.

Assessment
Russia, 1905-41 is one of the specified depth studies found in Paper 1, where you have a total of 2 hours to complete 3 questions. You must answer 2 questions from the core section of the paper and one question from a choice of two

questions on your chosen depth study. Therefore, you will answer one question on Russia, 1905-41 if this is your chosen depth study. The question is comprised of 3 sections; a, b, and c.

- Question a is worth 4 marks. This question will require you to describe key features of the time period. You will be asked to recall 2 relevant points and support them with details.

- Question b is worth 6 marks. This question will require you to explain a key event or development. You will need to identify two reasons, support those reasons with relevant factual detail and then explain how the reasons made the event occur.

- Question c is worth 10 marks. This question will require you to construct an argument to support and challenge an interpretation stated in the question. You will need to have a minimum of three explanations (two on one side and one on the other) in total, fully evaluate the argument and come to a justified conclusion. You will have the opportunity to show your ability to explain and analyse historical events using 2nd order concepts such as causation, consequence, change, continuity, similarity and difference.

Revision! A dreaded word. Everyone knows it's coming, everyone knows how much it helps with your exam performance, and everyone struggles to get started! We know you want to do the best you can in your IGCSEs, but schools aren't always clear on the best way to revise. This can leave students wondering:

- ✔ How should I plan my revision time?
- ✔ How can I beat procrastination?
- ✔ What methods should I use? Flash cards? Re-reading my notes? Highlighting?

Luckily, you no longer need to guess at the answers. Education researchers have looked at all the available revision studies, and the jury is in. They've come up with some key pointers on the best ways to revise, as well as some thoughts on popular revision methods that aren't so helpful. The next few pages will help you understand what we know about the best revision methods.

How can I beat procrastination?

This is an age-old question, and it applies to adults as well! Have a look at our top three tips below.

◎ Reward yourself

When we think a task we have to do is going to be boring, hard or uncomfortable, we often put if off and do something more 'fun' instead. But we often don't really enjoy the 'fun' activity because we feel guilty about avoiding what we should be doing. Instead, get your work done and promise yourself a reward after you complete it. Whatever treat you choose will seem all the sweeter, and you'll feel proud for doing something you found difficult. Just do it!

◎ Just do it!

We tend to procrastinate when we think the task we have to do is going to be difficult or dull. The funny thing is, the most uncomfortable part is usually making ourselves sit down and start it in the first place. Once you begin, it's usually not nearly as bad as you anticipated.

◎ Pomodoro technique

The pomodoro technique helps you trick your brain by telling it you only have to focus for a short time. Set a timer for 20 minutes and focus that whole period on your revision. Turn off your phone, clear your desk, and work. At the end of the 20 minutes, you get to take a break for five. Then, do another 20 minutes. You'll usually find your rhythm and it becomes easier to carry on because it's only for a short, defined chunk of time.

Spaced practice

We tend to arrange our revision into big blocks. For example, you might tell yourself: "This week I'll do all my revision for the Cold War, then next week I'll do the Medicine Through Time unit."

This is called **massed practice**, because all revision for a single topic is done as one big mass.

But there's a better way! Try **spaced practice** instead. Instead of putting all revision sessions for one topic into a single block, space them out. See the example below for how it works.

This means planning ahead, rather than leaving revision to the last minute - but the evidence strongly suggests it's worth it. You'll remember much more from your revision if you use **spaced practice** rather than organising it into big blocks. Whichever method you choose, though, remember to reward yourself with breaks.

Spaced practice (more effective):

week 1	week 2	week 3	week 4
Topic 1	Topic 1	Topic 1	Topic 1
Topic 2	Topic 2	Topic 2	Topic 2
Topic 3	Topic 3	Topic 3	Topic 3
Topic 4	Topic 4	Topic 4	Topic 4

Massed practice (less effective)

week 1	week 2	week 3	week 4
Topic 1	Topic 2	Topic 3	Topic 4

Quizzes, amazing exam preparation tools and more at GCSEHistory.com

What methods should I use to revise?

Self-testing/flash cards	Self explanation/mind-mapping

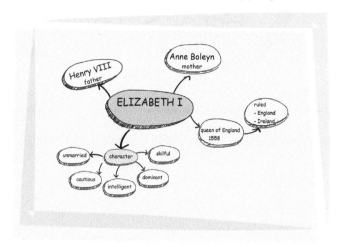

The research shows a clear winner for revision methods - **self-testing**. A good way to do this is with **flash cards**. Flash cards are really useful for helping you recall short – but important – pieces of information, like names and dates.

Side A - question

Side B - answer

Write questions on one side of the cards, and the answers on the back. This makes answering the questions and then testing yourself easy. Put all the cards you get right in a pile to one side, and only repeat the test with the ones you got wrong - this will force you to work on your weaker areas.

pile with right answers

pile with wrong answers

As this book has a quiz question structure itself, you can use it for this technique.

Another good revision method is **self-explanation**. This is where you explain how and why one piece of information from your course linked with another piece.

This can be done with **mind-maps**, where you draw the links and then write explanations for how they connect. For example, President Truman is connected with anti-communism because of the Truman Doctrine.

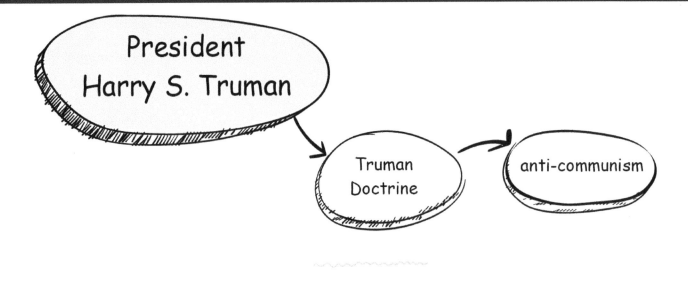

Review	Self-Test	Apply

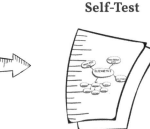
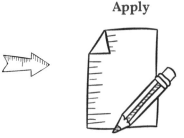

Start by highlighting or re-reading to create your flashcards for self-testing.	Test yourself with flash cards. Make mind maps to explain the concepts.	Apply your knowledge on practice exam questions.

Which revision techniques should I be cautious about?

Highlighting and **re-reading** are not necessarily bad strategies - but the research does say they're less effective than flash cards and mind-maps.

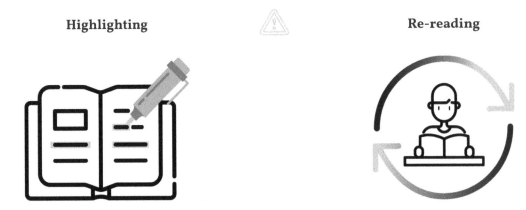

Highlighting   **Re-reading**

If you do use these methods, make sure they are **the first step to creating flash cards**. Really engage with the material as you go, rather than switching to autopilot.

TIMELINE

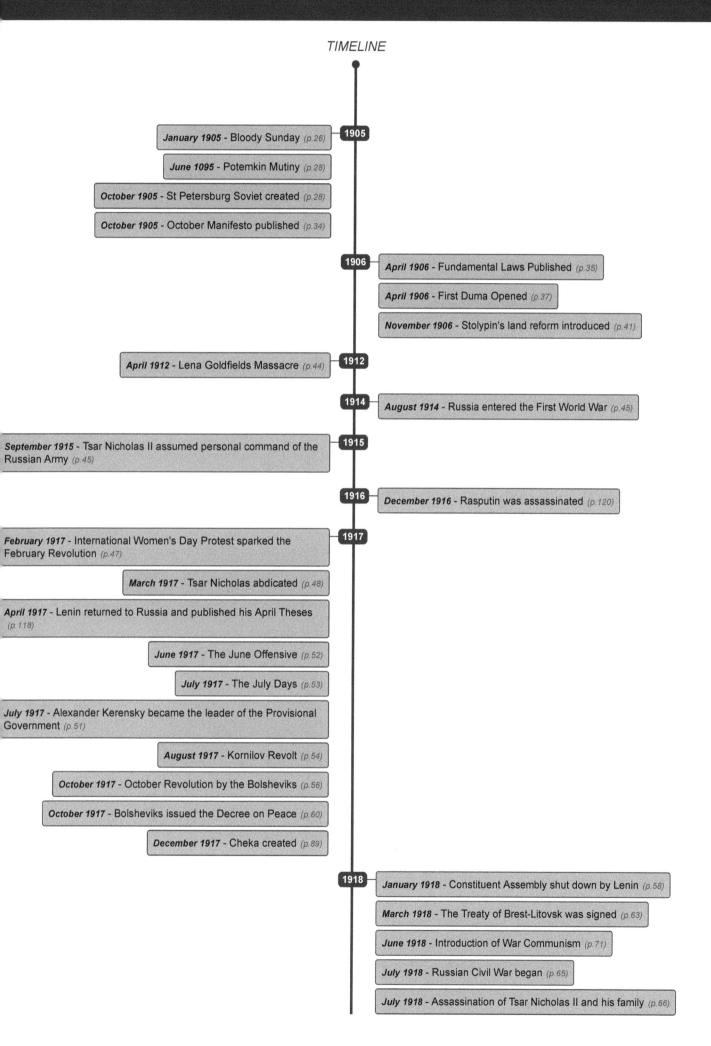

1905

January 1905 - Bloody Sunday *(p.26)*

June 1095 - Potemkin Mutiny *(p.28)*

October 1905 - St Petersburg Soviet created *(p.28)*

October 1905 - October Manifesto published *(p.34)*

1906

April 1906 - Fundamental Laws Published *(p.35)*

April 1906 - First Duma Opened *(p.37)*

November 1906 - Stolypin's land reform introduced *(p.41)*

1912

April 1912 - Lena Goldfields Massacre *(p.44)*

1914

August 1914 - Russia entered the First World War *(p.45)*

1915

September 1915 - Tsar Nicholas II assumed personal command of the Russian Army *(p.45)*

1916

December 1916 - Rasputin was assassinated *(p.120)*

1917

February 1917 - International Women's Day Protest sparked the February Revolution *(p.47)*

March 1917 - Tsar Nicholas abdicated *(p.48)*

April 1917 - Lenin returned to Russia and published his April Theses *(p.118)*

June 1917 - The June Offensive *(p.52)*

July 1917 - The July Days *(p.53)*

July 1917 - Alexander Kerensky became the leader of the Provisional Government *(p.51)*

August 1917 - Kornilov Revolt *(p.54)*

October 1917 - October Revolution by the Bolsheviks *(p.56)*

October 1917 - Bolsheviks issued the Decree on Peace *(p.60)*

December 1917 - Cheka created *(p.89)*

1918

January 1918 - Constituent Assembly shut down by Lenin *(p.58)*

March 1918 - The Treaty of Brest-Litovsk was signed *(p.63)*

June 1918 - Introduction of War Communism *(p.71)*

July 1918 - Russian Civil War began *(p.65)*

July 1918 - Assassination of Tsar Nicholas II and his family *(p.66)*

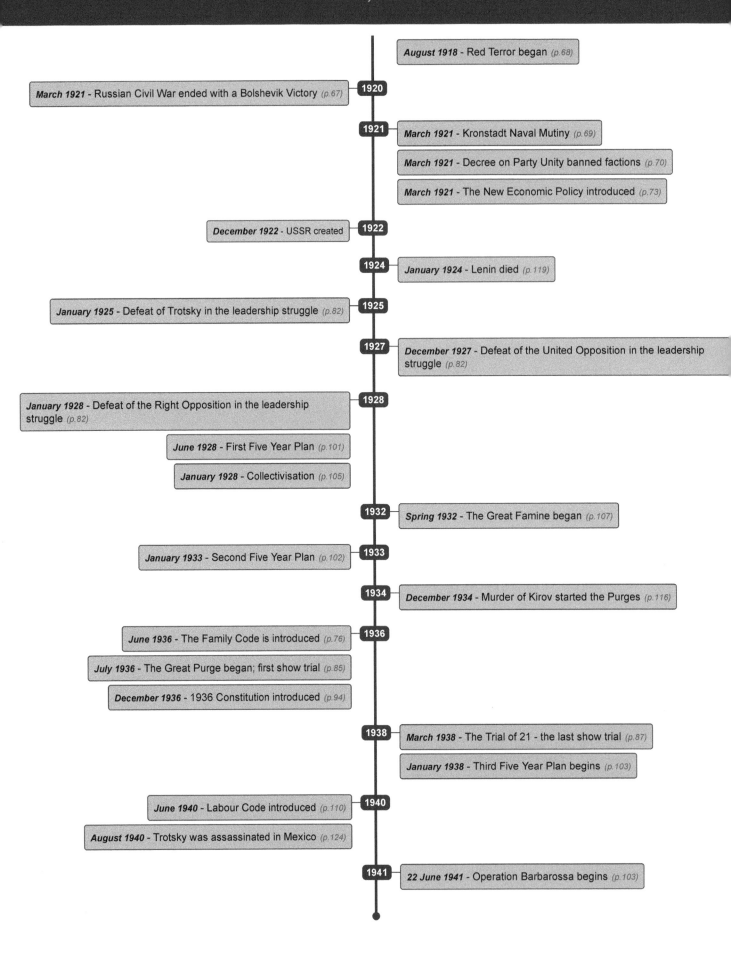

August 1918 - Red Terror began (p.68)

March 1921 - Russian Civil War ended with a Bolshevik Victory (p.67)

1920

1921

March 1921 - Kronstadt Naval Mutiny (p.69)

March 1921 - Decree on Party Unity banned factions (p.70)

March 1921 - The New Economic Policy introduced (p.73)

December 1922 - USSR created

1922

1924

January 1924 - Lenin died (p.119)

January 1925 - Defeat of Trotsky in the leadership struggle (p.82)

1925

1927

December 1927 - Defeat of the United Opposition in the leadership struggle (p.82)

January 1928 - Defeat of the Right Opposition in the leadership struggle (p.82)

1928

June 1928 - First Five Year Plan (p.101)

January 1928 - Collectivisation (p.105)

1932

Spring 1932 - The Great Famine began (p.107)

January 1933 - Second Five Year Plan (p.102)

1933

1934

December 1934 - Murder of Kirov started the Purges (p.116)

June 1936 - The Family Code is introduced (p.76)

1936

July 1936 - The Great Purge began; first show trial (p.85)

December 1936 - 1936 Constitution introduced (p.94)

1938

March 1938 - The Trial of 21 - the last show trial (p.87)

January 1938 - Third Five Year Plan begins (p.103)

June 1940 - Labour Code introduced (p.110)

1940

August 1940 - Trotsky was assassinated in Mexico (p.124)

1941

22 June 1941 - Operation Barbarossa begins (p.103)

INTRODUCTION TO RUSSIA IN THE EARLY 1900S

Churchill described Russia as: 'A riddle wrapped in a mystery inside an enigma.'

What was Russia like in the early 1900s?

In the early 1900s, Russia was an enormous empire which was economically and agriculturally backwards. It was ruled by an autocratic tsar *(p. 19)*, who had absolute power, and suppressed all opposition.

How many ethnic groups lived in Russia in the early 1900s?

Russia had approximately 130 ethnic groups, who spoke over 100 different languages.

How big was Russia in the early 1900s?

In the early 1900s, Russia was an empire that stretched 6,000 miles, from the Baltic to the Pacific and from the Arctic down to central Asia.

Which countries did Russia border in the early 1900s?

Russia shared a border with the German Empire in Europe and China in the Far East, as well as Finland in the north an Afghanistan in the south.

What geographical problems did Russia have in the early 1900s?

The geographical size of Russia causes 6 main problems:

- ☑ Due to the size of the country, certain areas were difficult to control as they were far away from the tsarist capital, S Petersburg.
- ☑ Communication across the country was poor, leading some areas to be divided and detached.
- ☑ There were a lack of railways and useable roads.
- ☑ A large amount of land was unsuitable for farming.
- ☑ The peasants used backward and inefficient agricultural methods.
- ☑ With an increasing population, land was in short supply.

What type of government did Russia have in the early 1900s?

There were 6 key features of tsarist government:

- ☑ The tsars were emperors who ruled with absolute power. Their power was justified by the belief that they possessed the divine right to rule.
- ☑ There was an Imperial Council who advised the tsar *(p. 19)*, whose members came from the nobility. The tsar appointed or dismissed its members, therefore the nobles were often corrupt and more interested in securing their position in the Imperial Council than providing balanced advice.
- ☑ There was a Committee of Ministers who ran 13 different departments (increased to 14 in 1900). The ministers were appointed by the tsar *(p. 19)* and their decisions needed his approval.
- ☑ There was a massive bureaucracy to run such a huge country. It was slow and often corrupt.
- ☑ Russia was divided into 117 different provinces which were run by the nobles. The governors of the provinces were responsible for enforcing the tsar's *(p. 19)* laws, which they could do with some degree of independence.
- ☑ It relied on the Imperial Army, the Russian Orthodox Church and the police to keep control.

How developed was industry in Russia in the early 1900s?

There were 6 main issues with Russia's level of industrialisation:

- ☑ It had a low-level of industry but it was growing quickly. By 1914, Russia was the world's 4th largest producer of coa pig iron and steel.

- ☑ Its banking system was backwards and could not support the investment needed to modernise the country.
- ☑ It lacked workers for new industries as many peasants were tied to their villages because of the debts they owed to their landlords.
- ☑ There was extreme poverty in Russia, therefore there was little demand for manufactured goods making investment for modernisation very difficult.
- ☑ The level of industrialisation was uneven across the empire. The industrial cities tended to be in the western parts of Russia.
- ☑ It lacked a developed transport network. There were few paved roads and although railways were developing, they were inadequate for helping Russia modernise.

What was farming like in Russia in the early 1900s?

There were 6 main issues with Russian agriculture:

- ☑ Agriculture was backward with little use of modern technology. Most peasants were subsistence farmers who mainly used traditional methods of farming because they had little to no education or opportunity to modernise.
- ☑ The peasants were emancipated in 1861, which meant they were free from serfdom. In practice, serfdom was replaced with debt slavery, forcing the peasants to take on loans in order to buy back their land.
- ☑ The Russian countryside experienced frequent famines and crop failures, leading to food shortages and starvation.
- ☑ The government failed to successfully deal with famines through a combination of the tsar's *(p.19)* indifference to suffering, poor infrastructure, local corruption and the nobles' mismanagement of the land.
- ☑ Most peasants were illiterate, poorly informed and resistant to change.
- ☑ The village commune, or mir, controlled how the peasants farmed and on which land they farmed. The mir allocated small strips of land to village peasants which was very often an ineffective and unproductive way to farm.

What were conditions like in Russia in the early 1900s?

By the 1900s, the living and working conditions in Russian town were terrible for 3 main reasons:

- ☑ Workers usually shared filthy rooms in block-style buildings.
- ☑ There could be up to 10 people sharing a room in these buildings, including men, women and children.
- ☑ Although working days were officially limited to 11 hours per day, the average working day was 15-16 hours.

What were the main religions of Russia in the early 1900s?

In the early 1900s, the 3 main religions were:

- ☑ Russian Orthodox, a form of Christianity, and the official state religion of Russia.
- ☑ Judaism. There were about 5 million Jews.
- ☑ Islam. There were about 23 million Muslims.

What role did the Church play in Russia in the early 1900s?

The Russian Orthodox Church played a very important role in Russia in 4 main ways:

- ☑ It taught the Russian people to love and obey the tsar *(p.19)* as the 'Little Father'.
- ☑ It underpinned the tsarist government as many Church leaders were from the aristocratic class of Russia's rulers who owned vast country estates.
- ☑ It was very conservative in nature and used its influence to block any change in Russia that might upset its position in society.
- ☑ It played a large role in education by teaching children to show loyalty to the tsar *(p.19)*, his officials, and the Church.

What different social classes existed in Russia in the early 1900s?

There were 7 different groups that made up Russian society by the late 1800s:

- ☑ The aristocrats made up about 1% of the population but owned 25% of the land.

- The clergy made up 0.5% of the population.
- The middle class of small bankers, merchants and professionals made up about 0.5% of the population.
- There was a class called 'urbanities' which consisted of small tradesmen, shopkeepers, white collar workers and artisans that made up 11% of the population.
- Cossacks made up about 2.3% of the population.
- The peasants made up about 80% of the population, an overwhelming majority, and were exceptionally poor and illiterate.
- About 8% was made up of other groups.

 ### What different nationalities made up Russia in the early 1900s?

In the early 1900s, Russia was made up of several different nationalities. The 5 main ones were:

- Slavs (including Belarusians, Russians, and Ukrainians).
- Poles.
- Asians.
- Germans.
- Latvians, Estonians and Lithuanians.

DID YOU KNOW?

3 facts about Russia:
- ✔ Great Britain could fit within the borders of the Russian Empire almost 100 times.
- ✔ The temperature could range from -60C in the winter to 40C in the summer.
- ✔ Northern Siberia might only be frost-free for 2 months a year.

THE RUSSIAN CALENDAR

Julius Caesar brought in the Julian calendar in 45BC.

What happened to the Russian calendar?
Russia has used two different calendars in the last 100 years: the Julian calendar and the Gregorian calendar.

When did the calendar change in Russia?
The old-style Julian calendar was replaced by the Gregorian calendar in January 1918.

What difference did the change to the Russian calendar make?
There were 2 main changes:

- The change from the Julian to the Gregorian calendar meant the loss of 13 days.
- Events that occurred before January 1918 have two dates. For example, the Bolshevik *(p.32)* Revolution occurred on 7th November, 1918 under the Gregorian calendar and on 25th October under the old Julian calendar.

TSARIST RULE

'I shall never, under any circumstances, agree to a representative form of government because I consider it harmful to the people whom God has entrusted to my care.' - Tsar Nicholas II, 1905

Who were the tsars?

The tsars were the kings or emperors who ruled Russia. They were autocrats which meant they had absolute power and could make any decision they liked. The position of the tsar was passed down the royal family from father to son.

Who helped the tsars govern Russia?

The tsars relied on the 5 key groups or organisations to rule Russia:

- ☑ Aristocratic ministers gave the tsars advice.
- ☑ The Russian Orthodox Church would support the tsars.
- ☑ The secret police, called the Okhrana, would crush any opposition.
- ☑ The army and navy swore an oath of loyalty to the tsar. The army could be used to crush any opposition.
- ☑ The zemstvos, or locally elected assemblies, set up to administer local affairs which were controlled by aristocrats.

How did the tsars control the countryside?

There were 4 key ways in which the tsars controlled the peasants:

- ☑ The peasants were freed in 1861 and were no longer serfs. However, they were in debt to the landowners because of this.
- ☑ A mir, or village commune, controlled the peasants.
- ☑ Law and order in the countryside was in the hands of the nobles.
- ☑ The zemstvos, or locally elected assemblies, were also controlled by the nobles.

How did the tsars select their ministers?

The tsars selected their ministers from 2 main groups:

- ☑ The aristocracy who were the people in the highest social class in Russia - they had land, money and power.
- ☑ The most senior officials in the Russian Orthodox Church.

What were the tsars responsible for?

The tsar was in charge of everything in the country. He had authority over the Church, all laws, taxation, the army and the navy.

TSAR NICHOLAS II

Tsar Nicholas was ill-equipped to rule Russia.

Who was Tsar Nicholas II?

Tsar Nicholas II was the last tsar *(p. 19)* of Russia. He was a part of the Romanov royal family that had ruled the nation since 1613.

When did Tsar Nicholas II rule Russia?

Tsar Nicholas II ruled Russia from 1894 to 1917.

How did Tsar Nicholas II rule Russia?

Nicholas II was an autocrat who had absolute power to do what he wanted.

Who helped Tsar Nicholas II to rule Russia?

Nicholas II relied on the following 4 institutions or organisations to rule Russia:

- ☑ The aristocracy.
- ☑ The Okhrana (secret police).
- ☑ The army.
- ☑ The Russian Orthodox Church.

What was Tsar Nicholas II like?

Nicholas II's rule of Russia was problematic for 5 main reasons:

- ☑ He had not been prepared for what the role would entail.
- ☑ He was a poor decision-maker and often procrastinated when faced with difficult decisions.
- ☑ His own lack of ability meant he was often jealous of his ministers. This created distrust and tension.
- ☑ He was very conservative by nature and determined to uphold his autocratic rule at all costs.
- ☑ His marriage to Alexandra Feodorovna, a German princess, led to problems as she became unpopular during the First World War. She made grave errors of judgement as the regent of Russia, a role she held while Nicholas commanded troops at the front.

What problems did Tsar Nicholas II face as the leader of Russia?

There were 5 main problems that Nicholas II faced as the ruler of Russia:

- ☑ Ensuring Russia was ruled effectively and efficiently.
- ☑ Modernising agriculture to become more productive, ensuring there were food surpluses to sell abroad. This gained money that was invested in the economy.

- Modernising Russian industry so that it could compete with Britain, Germany and the USA, and remain a great power.
- Reducing social and political unrest as different groups demanded reform.
- Ensuring Russian security in Europe and Asia as the international situation deteriorated, particularly with Japan, Germany and the Austro-Hungarian Empire.

What was Tsar Nicholas II's policy of Russification?

Russification *(p.42)* was a policy implemented by the tsars to force non-Russian minorities to partake in Russian culture and language. Due to this policy, discrimination against non-Russians became more open. This led to an increase in minority-based opposition to the tsars.

How did Tsar Nicholas II deal with opposition to his rule?

Tsar Nicholas II dealt with opposition to his rule in 5 key ways:

- He used the Okhrana, or secret police, to keep watch on suspected revolutionaries. Undercover agents would spy on groups.
- Revolutionaries and terrorists were prosecuted in court and either executed or exiled. Many executions were public to create fear.
- Government censorship of books and newspapers stopped the spread of any radical ideas that could undermine the tsarist government.
- When there were uprisings, such as Bloody Sunday in 1905, he used the army to crush the protesters.
- He brought in some reforms in an attempt to make some concessions to discontented groups, such as the reforms in his October Manifesto *(p.34)* in 1905.

Why was Tsar Nicholas II important?

There were 6 key events during Nicholas II's reign:

- His government was not viewed favourably because it failed to improve the lives of ordinary citizens and failed to reform.
- Russia was humiliated when it was defeated in the Russo-Japanese War *(p.25)*, 1904-05.
- Russia did very badly during the First World War and its people suffered as a result.
- There were several revolutions against his rule; one in 1905 and one in February 1917.
- He was forced to abdicate in March 1917.
- He was eventually executed by the Bolsheviks *(p.32)* during the Russian Civil War *(p.65)*.

How successful was Tsar Nicholas II in ruling Russia?

Tsar Nicholas II's government had 4 main successes:

- He managed to stay in power after the 1905 Revolution (until the February 1917 Revolution) and maintain a predominantly autocratic government.
- Some political reforms were brought in after the 1905 Revolution including the creation of the State Duma *(p.36)* (a parliament), voting rights and legalisation of political parties.
- Some economic reforms were introduced by Pyotr Stolypin to improve the working conditions of industrial workers.
- There was some economic development in terms of greater industrialisation. For example, there was a 50% increase in iron and steel production before the First World War.

How did Tsar Nicholas II fail?

Tsar Nicholas II's government failed in 5 key ways:

- He was a poor military leader and failed to defend Russia from her enemies. Russia was defeated in the Russo-Japanese War *(p.25)* and was doing incredibly badly in the First World War when he was forced to abdicate.

- ☑ He failed to bring in real political reforms to make Russia more democratic and this failure created even more political opposition.
- ☑ He failed to improve agriculture so there wasn't enough food for the growing population.
- ☑ He was a poor political leader, weak at ruling the country, who made poor decisions.
- ☑ Living and working conditions for workers and peasants did not improve; their wages stayed low while the cost of living rose.

 When did Tsar Nicholas II die?

Nicholas II died on 17th July, 1918.

 How did Tsar Nicholas II die?

The Bolsheviks *(p.32)* executed Tsar Nicholas II and his family by firing squad. Their bodies were then disposed of down a well.

DID YOU KNOW?

Tsar Nicholas II wrote in his diary:

'What is going to happen to me and all of Russia? I am not prepared to be a Tsar. I never wanted to become one. I know nothing of the business of ruling.'

TSARIST POLICE STATE

The tsarist form of government relied on the suppression of the police, army and church to rule.

 What was the tsarist police state?

The tsarist police state was how the tsars, like Nicholas II, ruled Russia. They used the police, the law, the courts, and censorship to control the people.

 What was the role of censorship in the tsarist police state?

The tsarist government banned radical ideas from being printed. All books and newspapers were censored.

 What was the Okhrana's role in the tsarist police state?

The Okhrana were the state secret police. They spied on people suspected of being revolutionaries or opposed to the regime.

 How were people who opposed the tsar punished in the tsarist police state?

People who were accused of opposing the tsarist regime were put in prison, exiled to Siberia, or executed.

DID YOU KNOW?

The Cossacks were mounted soldiers relied on by the tsars to suppress rebellions.

They played an important role in crushing the 1905 Revolution but turned against the tsar in the February 1917 Revolution to side with the protesters.

DISCONTENT

Most social classes in Russia were discontented.

What were the reasons for discontent in Russia in 1905?

There were a range of political, economic, social, and military problems that were causing discontent and unhappiness among different social classes in tsarist Russia by 1905.

What caused discontent in tsarist Russia in 1905?

There were 6 key reasons for discontent in Russia in 1905:

- ☑ The peasants were exceptionally poor, wanted more land and wanted taxes to be reduced.
- ☑ Industrial workers were angry about their working and living conditions, low pay and the high unemployment rates.
- ☑ Middle class people were frustrated they had no say in how the country was run because it was an autocracy. They wanted more freedom, but were afraid of revolution.
- ☑ Non-Russians did not want to be ruled by Russians and wanted their independence.
- ☑ There were radical groups that wanted to overthrow the tsar *(p.19)* and give power to the workers or peasants.
- ☑ Many people hated the police and secret police because they curtailed their freedom.

What caused discontent in the countryside in Russia 1905?

The peasants were unhappy because they were suffering in 4 main ways:

- ☑ The peasants were exceptionally poor, most were subsistence farmers and they needed more land.
- ☑ There were many famines which affected the Russian Empire in the 1890s and 1901. Thousands of people died.
- ☑ The tsar *(p.19)* and his government did not deal very well with the famines and the peasants were angry.
- ☑ Many peasants were in debt. From 1861 they were no longer owned by the landowners but had to pay for their freedom.

What caused discontent in the middle classes in Russia in 1905?

There were 4 main reasons the middle class was unhappy:

- ☑ Many wanted political reforms such as the freedom of speech or the right to vote which had been granted in other European countries.
- ☑ Many wanted to remove the tsar *(p.19)* and have a written constitution which would give everyone equal rights.
- ☑ Many were terrified of the revolutionary political groups that had developed in Russia as the middle class would lose out if a revolution occurred.
- ☑ They were frustrated with Tsar Nicholas II's *(p.20)* unwillingness to implement political reform.

What caused discontent in the industrial workers in tsarist Russia?

There were 4 main reasons why the industrial workers were unhappy:

- ☑ Their working conditions were awful and dangerous.
- ☑ Their pay was very poor.
- ☑ Their living conditions were terrible as their pay was so low they could not afford anywhere better to live and often lived in overcrowded conditions.
- ☑ Workers suffered from illnesses and often became alcoholics as a result of their living conditions.

Why were non-Russians unhappy in tsarist Russia?

There were 3 key reasons why non-Russians were unhappy:

- ☑ The Russian Empire contained some 19 different nationalities in the areas conquered by the tsars over the years. Those areas wanted their independence.
- ☑ Russia forced 'Russification (p.42)' on the non-Russian areas.
- ☑ Russian people got preferential treatment e.g. Russians were given jobs in the local government in preference to the local people.

How did discontent relate to political opposition in tsarist Russia?

There were 3 main issues with political opposition:

- ☑ Political parties were illegal so people could not express their political views.
- ☑ Despite being illegal, political groups that opposed the tsarist regime were set up. For example, groups included the Populists, Social Democrats, Social Revolutionaries, the Mensheviks and the Bolsheviks (p.32).
- ☑ Some groups like the Social Revolutionaries, Social Democrats, the Mensheviks and the Bolsheviks (p.32) wanted to completely remove the tsarist regime through revolution.

DID YOU KNOW?

Tsar Alexander II claimed: 'It is not difficult to rule Russia, but it is useless.'

POLITICAL OPPOSITION TO THE TSAR

Political opposition to the tsarist form of government had been growing since the mid-1800s.

What political opposition was there to Tsar Nicholas II?

Opposition to Tsar Nicholas II was growing because he would not allow political reform and did not improve living conditions.

When was there political opposition to Tsar Nicholas II?

Opposition to the tsarist regime was growing throughout the 1800s and early 1900s, although political parties were illegal until October 1905.

Why was there political opposition to Tsar Nicholas II?

Political opposition to Nicholas II was growing because of 3 key reasons:

- ☑ Some groups wanted to limit the power of Nicholas II.
- ☑ Some wanted radical change and to completely remove Nicholas II from power.
- ☑ Most groups wanted to see reforms brought in to improve the social, economic, and political conditions in Russia.

Who was the political opposition to Tsar Nicholas II?

There were several different groups that opposed Nicholas II such as the Liberals (split into the Kadets and the Octobrists), the Socialist Revolutionary Party (p.30), and the Social Democratic Party (p.32).

Why did Tsar Nicholas II face opposition from the Social Democratic Party?

The Social Democratic Party (p.32) was set up in 1898 and:

- ☑ Believed in communism and the ideas of Karl Marx.
- ☑ Wanted a revolution to get rid of Nicholas II and the tsarist government.

- Believed in giving power to the workers.
- They wanted to establish a communist state.
- In 1903 they split into the moderate Mensheviks and the more revolutionary Bolsheviks. *(p.32)*

 Why did Tsar Nicholas II face opposition from Socialist Revolutionary Party?

The Socialist Revolutionary Party *(p.30)* wanted to end the tsarist regime:

- Some believed in using terrorism to achieve this and assassinated Tsar *(p.19)* Alexander II in 1881. They were responsible for around 2,000 assassinations between 1901 and 1905.
- Others believed in working with other political groups to improve working and living conditions.

 Why did Tsar Nicholas II face opposition from the Liberals?

Some groups such as the Kadets wanted a constitutional government in which the tsar *(p.19)* remained as the head of state. However, his power was to be limited by a constitution, and there would be a democratically elected government.

DID YOU KNOW?

Political discontent had increased over many years when Nicholas became tsar.

Nicholas II's own grandfather, Tsar Alexander II, was assassinated in 1881 and there were several attempts on the life of his father, Tsar Alexander III.

THE RUSSO-JAPANESE WAR, 1904-05

The Russo-Japanese War of 1904-05 was a national humiliation for Russia.

 What was the Russo-Japanese War?

The Russo-Japanese War was a conflict between the Russian Empire, ruled by Tsar Nicholas II *(p.20)*, and Imperial Japan under Emperor Meiji.

 When was the Russo-Japanese War?

The Russo-Japanese War began on 8th February, 1904, and ended on 5th September (23rd August, Old Style), 1905.

 Why did the Russo-Japanese War happen?

There were 5 key causes of the Russo-Japanese War:

- Russia wanted to expand its territory in China in an area called Manchuria. This brought Russia into conflict with Japan, which was trying to do the same.
- Tsar Nicholas II *(p.20)* wanted a 'short, swift victorious' war to reduce opposition at home which was growing due to deteriorating conditions.
- Russia needed ports that could be used all year as its existing ports froze over in winter.
- The Russians did not believe Japan, as an Asian nation, would be able to beat them as they considered them inferior.
- Russia was considering expanding the Trans-Siberian Railway into Manchuria. The Japanese saw that as a threat to their position in Korea.

What happened during the Russo-Japanese War?

There were 6 key events of the war:

☑ In January 1904, Port Arthur, a Russian naval base, was attacked by the Japanese.

☑ In February 1905, Russia was defeated in the Battle of Mukden and surrendered it to Japan.

☑ In May 1905, at the Battle of Tsushima, the Russian Baltic fleet was defeated by the Japanese navy.

☑ In August 1905, the Japanese won a major land battle in the Battle of Liaoyang despite having a smaller force.

☑ In January 1905, Port Arthur surrendered to the Japanese.

☑ In September 1905, both sides formally ended the war when they signed the Treaty of Portsmouth.

What was the significance of the Russo-Japanese War for Russia?

Russia's defeat in the Russo-Japanese War was significant for 4 reasons:

☑ Tsar Nicholas II *(p.20)* was blamed for the humiliation of being defeated by Japan, which had been considered a lesser power.

☑ The military defeats in the war helped cause the mutiny on the Battleship Potemkin in June 1905.

☑ Fighting the war put even more strain on the government's resources and diverted much-needed grain and fuel away from the people, creating even more discontent.

☑ It was a key trigger of the 1905 Revolution and Bloody Sunday incident.

DID YOU KNOW?

Japan's navy included many British-built battleships.

BLOODY SUNDAY, 1905

Bloody Sunday in 1905 seriously undermined Tsar Nicholas II's authority.

 What was Bloody Sunday?

Bloody Sunday is the name of a massacre that happened in St Petersburg. Around 200 people were killed.

 When was Bloody Sunday?

Bloody Sunday happened on Sunday, 22nd January, 1905 (9th January, Old Style).

 Why did Bloody Sunday happen in 1905?

There were 5 key reasons for the protest:

☑ The protesters wanted a constitution which would protect the rights of the people.

☑ They marched to present a petition to Tsar Nicholas II *(p.20)* complaining about working conditions.

☑ They wanted to be able to set up trade unions to protect the rights of workers.

☑ They wanted to only work eight hours a day.

☑ They wanted a minimum wage of one rouble per day.

 What happened during Bloody Sunday?

The 5 key events of Bloody Sunday were:

- ☑ A large group of protesters, made up of workers and their families, gathered in St Petersburg led by Father Gapon.
- ☑ Soldiers blocked the protesters' route to the tsar's *(p. 19)* palace.
- ☑ Warning shots were fired.
- ☑ Mounted Cossacks attacked the protesters and then the soldiers fired at the crowd.
- ☑ 200 people died and 800 were wounded.

What was the importance of Bloody Sunday in Russia?

The Bloody Sunday massacre encouraged 4 key further protests:

- ☑ The Potemkin mutiny in June 1905.
- ☑ Peasant riots across Russia between 1905 and 1907.
- ☑ Strikes across Russia by workers.
- ☑ The creation of soviets, or workers' councils.

Why did Tsar Nicholas II survive the consequences of Bloody Sunday?

There are 6 key reasons Nicholas II survived Bloody Sunday:

- ☑ The army stayed loyal to him and crushed the demonstration.
- ☑ He issued the October Manifesto *(p. 34)* which won over the middle class and liberals as it appeared to give them power through the setting up of a State Duma *(p. 36)*, or parliament.
- ☑ Pyotr Stolypin, as Minister of the Interior and then the Prime Minister, used the army and police to crush all political opposition.
- ☑ Any person suspected of being a revolutionary was arrested and imprisoned.
- ☑ Newspapers and trade unions were closed.
- ☑ The opposition was split between different groups such as workers, sailors, peasants and minority nationalities that wanted different things.

DID YOU KNOW?

There was much criticism of Tsar Nicholas II's suppression of the demonstrators.

America, Britain and France all condemned his actions.

THE 1905 REVOLUTION

Tsar Nicholas II survived the upheaval of the 1905 Revolution by satisfying some of the key discontented groups.

What was the Russian Revolution of 1905?

Russia faced massive social and political unrest during the Revolution of 1905. Some of this was directed at the government.

When was the Russian Revolution of 1905?

The Russian Revolution of 1905 started on 22nd January that year. Unrest lasted until 1907.

What caused the Russian Revolution of 1905?

There were 5 causes of the 1905 revolution:

☑ One long-term cause was discontent amongst the peasants because they were heavily taxed, incredibly poor, and suffered from famines and hunger on a regular basis.

☑ Another long-term cause was discontent among industrial workers because they had terrible working and living conditions and very low pay. Unemployment was rising in the early 1900s.

☑ A third long-term cause was the growth in political opposition to Nicholas II from different groups such as the country's different nationalities and political organisations, such as the Social Revolutionaries.

☑ An immediate cause was Russia's defeat in the Russo-Japanese War (p.25) of 1904-05. Tsar Nicholas II (p.20) was blamed for the defeat and lost support as a result.

☑ A major trigger cause was Bloody Sunday. On 22nd January, unarmed civilians led by Father Gapon were shot by tsarist soldiers in St Petersburg.

What events occurred during the 1905 Russian Revolution?

There were 7 key events during the 1905 revolution:

☑ There was a mutiny by sailors on the navy battleship Potemkin over poor quality food. This resulted in the deaths of some officers and sailors on 14th June, 1905.

☑ The Potemkin sailed to the port of Odessa where strikers and protesters showed their support for the sailors. There were riots, which Nicholas II ordered the army to stop. 1,000 people were shot dead.

☑ There were riots across Russia by peasants between 1905 and 1907. They burned their landlords' homes and created communes to share the land.

☑ Industrial workers announced a general strike between 20th September and 2nd October, 1905.

☑ The workers organised into soviets, or worker councils, in St Petersburg and Moscow by October 1905. These were elected councils which demanded better conditions. Leon Trotsky became the chairman of the St Petersburg Soviet.

☑ The government issued the October Manifesto (p.34) on 17th October. This granted civil rights, a parliament called a Duma (p.36), and promised new laws would be discussed.

☑ Unrest continued across the country which was quashed by the army. The most notable was the crushing of the Moscow Soviet uprising led by Social Democrats in December 1905, which resulted in over 1,000 people being killed.

What was the government's response to the 1905 Russian Revolution?

Nicholas II's government took 4 key actions:

☑ They crushed many of the protests. For example, the army shot the protesters in Odessa and in Moscow in December 1905, when the Moscow Soviet tried to organise an uprising.

☑ They closed down the soviets. For example, the St Petersburg Soviet was shut down in December 1905.

☑ The tsar (p.19) issued the October Manifesto (p.34) on 17th October, which granted civil rights, a parliament called a Duma (p.36), and promised new laws would be discussed by the new parliament.

☑ There was a harsh and violent crackdown on any opposition. There were arrests with many people exiled or put to death - more than 1000 people were executed between 1906 and 1907.

What was the outcome of the Russian Revolution of 1905?

There were 4 main results of the Revolution of 1905.

☑ Nicholas II and his government survived.

☑ The strikers and the revolutionaries were defeated.

☑ The October Manifesto (p.34) was published.

☑ A state Duma (p.36) was created.

Why did Nicholas II survive the 1905 Russian Revolution?

There were 3 key reasons Nicholas II survived the 1905 Revolution:

☑ The military, on the whole, still supported Nicholas II and crushed the uprisings.

☑ He made concessions which pleased the liberals and the middle classes; these changes were detailed in the October Manifesto *(p.34)*.

☑ The opposition was split between different groups that wanted different things.

DID YOU KNOW?

The 1925 film, 'Battleship Potemkin', directed by Sergei Eisenstein, tells the story of the 1905 mutiny which contributed to the revolution. Some consider it the greatest film of all time.

THE OCTOBRIST PARTY - OCTOBRISTS

The Octobrists were named after the October Manifesto which they supported.

Who were the Octobrists?

The Octobrist Party was a Russian political party with socially conservative, but constitutionally liberal views. It was created in November 1905.

When was the Octobrist Party set up?

The Octobrist Party existed from 1905 to 1917, when they were made illegal by the Bolshevik *(p.32)* Party.

Why was the Octobrist Party set up?

The Octobrist Party was set up after Tsar Nicholas II *(p.20)* issued his October Manifesto *(p.34)* to support the implementation of the changes the October Manifesto.

What were the views of the Octobrist Party?

The Octobrists had 2 key views:

☑ They believed in a limited constitutional monarchy in which the State Duma *(p.36)* passed laws but the tsar *(p.19)* kept his authority.

☑ They initially supported Stolypin's economic policies but became more critical because of his repressive policies.

What was the role of the Octobrist Party in the Duma?

The Octobrists played 4 main roles in the State Dumas:

☑ The Octobrists became the largest group in the third Duma *(p.38)* because Stolypin changed the voting laws in 1907.

☑ They supported Russia's entry into the First World War in 1914.

☑ They joined the Progressive Bloc in 1915 with the Kadets, or Constitutional Democratic Party *(p.31)*, which wanted more representative leadership and reform.

☑ They held several positions in the government during the First World War and the Dual Power of the Provisional Government *(p.50)* and the Petrograd Soviet *(p.49)* in 1917.

THE SOCIALIST REVOLUTIONARY PARTY

The Socialist Revolutionaries were prepared to use violence to achieve their aims.

What was the Socialist Revolutionary Party?

The Socialist Revolutionary Party was a Russian political party that wanted to end the tsarist regime - some of of its members were happy to use violence.

When was the Socialist Revolutionary Party important?

The Socialist Revolutionary Party was created in 1902 and made illegal by the Bolsheviks *(p.32)* in 1917.

What did the Socialist Revolutionary Party believe?

The Socialist Revolutionary Party believed in land reform, so there would be no private ownership of land. Instead, it would be held by the communes.

What tactics did the Socialist Revolutionary Party use?

The Socialist Revolutionary Party often committed political assassinations and used terrorist tactics.

THE TRUDOVIK PARTY

Trudovik means 'labour'; the Trudoviks were a political party representing peasant farmers.

What was the Trudovik Party?

The Trudovik Party was a Russian political party created in 1906 when the Socialist Revolutionary Party *(p.30)* refused to take part in the first Duma *(p.37)*.

Quizzes, amazing exam preparation tools and more at GCSEHistory.com

When was the Trudovik Party created?

The Trudovik Party was created in 1906 and was very important during the first and second Dumas of Russia because they won many seats. They were made illegal by the Bolsheviks *(p.32)* in 1917.

Why was the Trudovik Party created?

Some members of the Socialist Revolutionary Party *(p.30)* created a new party, the Trudoviks, because they opposed the party's decision to not participate in the first Duma *(p.37)*.

What were the views of the Trudovik Party?

The Trudovik Party's main belief was in land reform. It thought all land ownership should be in the hands of the peasants. They supported the Provisional Government *(p.50)*.

DID YOU KNOW?

Alexander Kerensky was a member of the Trudovik Party.

THE KADETS

The Constitutional Democratic Party, or Kadets, was made up of liberals mainly supported by the middle and upper classes.

Who were the Kadets?

The Kadets, or Constitutional Democratic Party, was a Russian political party established in 1906 that had liberal beliefs.

When was the Kadet Party important?

The Kadets, or Constitutional Democratic Party, was created in 1906 and made illegal by the Bolsheviks *(p.32)* in 1917. They were very important in the first Duma *(p.37)* as they were the largest party.

What did the Kadet Party believe?

The Kadets had 3 main beliefs:

- ☑ They wanted a constitutional monarchy similar to Britain.
- ☑ Universal, free and equal suffrage (voting rights).
- ☑ Land reform to favour the peasants but which compensated the landlords.

DID YOU KNOW?

The Kadets leader was Pavel Milyukov and Prince Lvov was one of their leading members.

THE SOCIAL DEMOCRATIC PARTY

The Social Democratic Party believed in communism.

Who were the Social Democratic Party?

The Russian Social Democratic Party was created in 1898 and followed Karl Marx's ideas about communist revolution.

When was the Social Democratic Party important?

The Social Democratic Party was important from its creation, in 1898, until it split into 2 separate parties in 1903.

What did the Social Democratic Party believe?

The Social Democratic Party believed in communism and the need for a revolution in Russia to overthrow the tsarist regime.

Why did the Social Democratic Party split?

The Social Democratic Party split in 1903 because there was a disagreement about how to achieve a communist revolution:

- ☑ The Mensheviks believed the revolution would only happen after Russia industrialised and created a large working class. This would take a long time.
- ☑ The Bolsheviks *(p.32)* believed that the revolution in Russia could happen more quickly if a small group of dedicated revolutionaries led the revolution and set up a dictatorship of the proletariat on behalf of the workers.

> **DID YOU KNOW?**
>
> Communism is a political ideology developed by Karl Marx.

THE BOLSHEVIK PARTY

'A revolution is 'made' directly by a minority.' - Trotsky, writing in 1938

Who were the Bolsheviks?

The Bolsheviks were founded by Vladimir Lenin and Alexander Bogdanov when the Social Democratic Party *(p.32)* split into two: the Bolsheviks and the Mensheviks. Bolshevik means 'majority' and Menshevik means 'minority'.

When was the Bolshevik party formed?

The Bolsheviks were formed in Brussels, Belgium, in 1903.

How many members did the Bolshevik party have?

At the beginning of 1917, they had just 23,000 members.

What did the Bolshevik party believe in?

The Bolsheviks had 5 main beliefs:

- ☑ In creating a communist society in which all private ownership of property, land and businesses would be abolished to benefit the workers.

Quizzes, amazing exam preparation tools and more at GCSEHistory.com

- ☑ The party should be run by a small dedicated group of revolutionaries who would lead the communist revolution.
- ☑ Russia was not ready for a communist revolution according to Marx's theory because it was not yet fully industrialised and the peasants and workers were not ready.
- ☑ The Bolsheviks would create a 'Dictatorship of the Proletariat' and rule on the workers' behalf.
- ☑ They refused to work with other political parties.

How were the beliefs of the Bolshevik party different to those of the Mensheviks?

There were 3 main differences between the Mensheviks' beliefs and those of the Bolsheviks:

- ☑ The Mensheviks were willing to work with other left-wing parties to bring about democracy, but the Bolsheviks were not.
- ☑ The Bolsheviks believed in forcing a revolution, whereas the Mensheviks believed in a more democratic approach to gaining power.
- ☑ The Mensheviks believed a liberal capitalist society would be a stepping stone to communism, whereas the Bolsheviks believed a small group leading a revolution by force was the way to achieve it.

DID YOU KNOW?

Trotsky was originally a Menshevik for a short time, before crossing over and allying himself with Lenin and the Bolsheviks.

THE MENSHEVIKS

Trotsky said to the Mensheviks in 1917: 'You are pitiful isolated individuals; you are bankrupts; your role is played out. Go where you belong from now on - into the dustbin of history!'

Who were the Mensheviks?

The Mensheviks were founded by Julius Martov when the Social Democratic Party *(p.32)* split into two: the Bolsheviks *(p.32)* and the Mensheviks. Bolshevik means 'majority' and Menshevik means 'minority'.

When were the Mensheviks created?

The Mensheviks were formed in Brussels, Belgium, in 1903.

What were the Mensheviks beliefs?

The Mensheviks had 5 key beliefs:

- ☑ In creating a communist society in which all private ownership of property, land and businesses would be abolished to benefit the workers.
- ☑ The communist revolution would only happen after Russia industrialised to create a large working class. This would take a long time.
- ☑ The party should be be democratic, rather than dominated by a 'revolutionary elite'.
- ☑ That the party should work with other political parties to achieve a liberal, capitalist society as the first step towards a communist revolution.
- ☑ They gained the support of the working class by promoting policies such as an eight hour working day.

How were the Mensheviks different to the Bolsheviks?

There were 3 main differences between the Mensheviks and the Bolsheviks *(p.32)*:

- They were willing to work with other left-wing parties to bring about democracy whereas the Bolsheviks (p.32) were not.
- They believed in a more democratic approach to gaining power whereas the Bolsheviks (p.32) believed in forcing a revolution.
- They believed that a liberal capitalist society would be a stepping stone to communism, unlike the Bolsheviks (p.32) who believed in a small group leading a revolution by force.

What was the role of the Mensheviks in the 1905 Revolution?

The Mensheviks played 3 main roles in the 1905 Revolution:

- They encouraged workers to set up councils or 'soviets'.
- They were crucial to the set up of the Petrograd Soviet (p.49).
- They played an active role in the state Dumas which were established by Tsar Nicholas II (p.20) in response to the 1905 Revolution.

What happened to the Mensheviks?

The Bolsheviks (p.32) suppressed the Mensheviks, along with all other political parties, and many Mensheviks went into exile.

DID YOU KNOW?

The Mensheviks became less popular after the October Revolution.

THE OCTOBER MANIFESTO, 1905

The October Manifesto seemed to be a compromise by Tsar Nicholas II but in reality he reamined the autocratic leader.

What was the October Manifesto?

The October Manifesto, or The Manifesto on the Improvement of the State Order, was published by Nicholas II's government and granted certain rights and freedoms to the people of Russia.

When was the October Manifesto published?

The October Manifesto was published on 30th October, 1905 (or 17th October, Old Style).

What was the reason for the October Manifesto?

Tsar Nicholas II (p.20) was forced to compromise after the uprisings of 1905. He laid out his reforms in the October Manifesto.

What did the October Manifesto contain?

Nicholas II granted 3 key things in the October Manifesto:

- A parliament, called a Duma (p.36), which would have elected representatives.
- Civil rights for all Russian citizens, including freedom of speech and the right to form political parties and trade unions.
- New laws would be discussed and approved by the Duma (p.36).

What were the results of the October Manifesto?

The publication of the October Manifesto led to 3 key results:

- ✅ An array of political parties were created such as the Octobrists, the Kadets, the Social Democratic Party *(p.32)* and others.

- ✅ Nicholas II passed the Fundamental Laws in April 1906 which established the Duma *(p.36)* and its powers. However, he deliberately limited the powers of the Duma so that it was little more than an advisory body.

- ✅ Many middle class people and liberals were very happy with the reforms the October Manifesto outlined.

DID YOU KNOW?

By offering certain concessions, Nicholas cleverly divided the discontented groups.

The liberal middle classes were satisfied with the new power that establishing the State Duma would give them, while peasants had been bought off by having their debts eased.

THE FUNDAMENTAL LAWS, 1906

The Fundamental Laws sharply curtailed the powers of the new State Duma.

What were the Fundamental Laws?

Tsar Nicholas II *(p.20)* set out his political reforms in the Fundamental Laws.

When were the Fundamental Laws made?

The Fundamental Laws were published in April 1906.

Why did Nicholas II pass the Fundamental Laws?

Tsar Nicholas II *(p.20)* published the Fundamental Laws to reestablish his control over the country after the 1905 Revolution forced him to make compromises in the October Manifesto *(p.34)*.

What did the Fundamental Laws state?

There were 6 key features of the Fundamental Laws:

- ✅ The establishment of the Duma *(p.36)*, which was made up of about 500 delegates, and details of how they would contribute to making laws.

- ✅ The tsar *(p.19)* could close the Duma *(p.36)* at any point.

- ✅ The tsar *(p.19)* could change the electoral system.

- ✅ The Duma's *(p.36)* powers would be limited by the creation of an upper house called the Imperial State Council. The tsar *(p.19)* would select half its members.

- ✅ The tsar *(p.19)* could veto any law the Duma *(p.36)* passed.

- ✅ The tsar *(p.19)* could pass any laws he wanted when the Duma *(p.36)* was not in session.

What was the result of Nicholas II passing the Fundamental Laws?

The result of Nicholas II passing the Fundamental Laws was that the powers of the Duma *(p.36)* were limited and he was back in control.

THE STATE DUMA

The State Duma was Russia's first elected parliament.

What was the Duma?

To please the liberals, Tsar Nicholas II *(p.20)* allowed a parliament called the Duma to be established. This was his main attempt to restore order following the 1905 Revolution.

When was the Duma created?

The Duma was established by Tsar Nicholas II *(p.20)* in his October Manifesto *(p.34)*, published on 30th October, 1905. After being dismissed for the first time in 1906 it was elected a further three times - twice in 1907 and once in 1912.

What was the Duma's purpose?

The Duma was a parliament which would confirm the laws of the Russian Empire.

What happened to the Duma during the First Word War?

The tsar *(p.19)* took over direct command of the army and dissolved the Duma in 1914. But the war didn't go according to plan and the Duma was recalled a year later. By 1917, it was a main source of opposition to the tsar.

What was Tsar Nicholas II's attitude towards the Duma?

Nicholas II's attitude towards the Duma was mixed:

- ☑ As an autocrat, he disliked the idea of sharing power with the people.
- ☑ He didn't really trust the people to have a say in how the country was run.
- ☑ He saw it as a threat so limited its powers through the Fundamental Laws of 1906.
- ☑ He did, at times, treat it seriously.
- ☑ He saw it primarily as an advisory body, and he made sure that he always had the final say.

FIRST DUMA, 1906

The opening of the first Duma was an historic event.

What was the first Duma?

The first Duma was the very first parliament in the Russian Empire during the reign of Tsar Nicholas II *(p.20)*. It was a historic moment because Russia had never before had an elected parliament.

When did the first Duma exist?

The first Duma existed between 27th April and 8th July, 1906.

What did the first Duma want?

The first Duma wanted 3 key reforms:

- ☑ Land reform, where more land would be taken from the landlords and distributed amongst the people.
- ☑ Political prisoners to be released.
- ☑ The Imperial State Council to be abolished.

Who sat in the first Duma?

The first Duma was made up of 4 main groups:

- ☑ Very few radical left-wing parties because most had boycotted the election.
- ☑ The moderate Constitutional Democrats (Kadets) had the most deputies.
- ☑ The Trudoviks (Labourites) had around 100 deputies.
- ☑ There were a number of smaller parties, including the Octobrists.

What was Nicholas II's reaction to the demands of the first Duma?

Nicholas II was horrified by the demands for reform because he saw them as too radical, so he dissolved the first Duma.

What was the result of Nicholas II dissolving the first Duma?

The liberals were very unhappy when Nicholas II dissolved the first Duma and shut it down. His actions increased their opposition to him.

DID YOU KNOW?

Tsar Nicholas II gave a speech to the delegates of the first Duma in the Winter Palace when it opened.

SECOND DUMA, 1907

The second Duma was just as radical as the short-lived first Duma.

What was the second Duma?

The second Duma was the second parliament while Nicholas II was the tsar *(p.19)* of Russia. It was very short-lived because of its radical demands.

When did the second Duma exist?

The second Duma existed between February and June in 1907.

What did the second Duma want?

The second Duma wanted 2 key reforms:

- ✅ It proposed radical change to the tsarist army.
- ✅ It opposed Stolypin's land reforms.

Who sat in the second Duma?

There were changes to which political parties were present in the second Duma:

- ✅ Some Kadets were not allowed to sit in the second Duma because they had criticised the government for closing the first one.
- ✅ There were more Octobrists and Social Revolutionaries, and 220 socialists altogether.

What was Nicholas II's reaction to the demands of the second Duma?

Some Kadets were not allowed to sit in the second Duma because they had criticised the government for closing the first one.

What was result of Nicholas II dissolving the second Duma?

The political parties began to realise the Duma *(p.36)* did not have any real power and could not bring about any reform.

DID YOU KNOW?

The second Duma was closed down because it was seen as too radical.

As a result, Stolypin changed the rules as to who had the right to vote.

THIRD DUMA, 1907 TO 1912

The third Duma was more supportive of the Tsar because of changes to the electoral laws.

What was the third Duma?

The third Duma was the third parliament while Nicholas II was the Tsar *(p.19)* of Russia.

When did the third Duma exist?

The third Duma was in session between November 1907 and June 1912.

What laws did the third Duma pass?

The third Duma cooperated with, and supported Nicholas II, far more than the previous two. This meant more laws proposed by Stolypin were passed in the following areas:

- ✅ Land reform.
- ✅ Social welfare measures.

☑ Improvements to the military.

Who sat in the third Duma?

The third Duma:

☑ Was affected by Prime Minister Stolypin's alteration of the electoral system, which gave landowners more voting power so only the richest third of the population could vote.

☑ Saw more pro-tsar conservative deputies elected, such as the Octobrists, so they and other conservatives had most of the seats.

☑ Had fewer deputies from non-Russian regions.

What was the response of the political parties to the third Duma?

There were 2 key responses to the changes made to the electoral system and the impact this had on the third Duma:

☑ The liberals were very unhappy as they realised Nicholas II and his government would never allow true democracy or give up their autocratic powers.

☑ The more radical parties were angered by the changes and more groups began to favour revolution.

DID YOU KNOW?

The third Duma was the only State Duma to last its full five-year term.

FOURTH DUMA, 1912 TO 1917

The fourth and final Duma failed to compel Tsar Nicholas bring in political reforms.

What was the fourth Duma?

The fourth Duma was the fourth and final parliament while Nicholas II was the Tsar *(p.19)* of Russia.

When did the fourth Duma exist?

The fourth Duma was in session between November 1912 and February 1917. It was finally closed in October 1917.

Who sat in the fourth Duma?

The fourth Duma was elected using the altered electoral system which gave the richest third of the population more voting power. It was dominated by conservatives, especially the nationalists and right-wing parties.

What did the fourth Duma do?

The fourth Duma faced 3 main problems:

☑ It struggled to make much of a difference during the crisis of the First World War.

☑ In 1915, a progressive bloc formed, consisting of the centre parties, which tried to make the government and Nicholas II more responsive to the people. It failed.

☑ One new member, Alexander Kerensky, would become important after the February 1917 revolution.

When was the fourth Duma shut down?

The fourth Duma opened and closed several times between 1912 and 1917. It was eventually dissolved in February 1917. However, members of the fourth Duma continued to run the country as a part of the Provisional Government *(p.50)* so was finally closed in October 1917.

DID YOU KNOW?

The State Dumas met in the Tauride Palace in St Petersburg.

The palace was also used by the Provisional Government and the Petrograd Soviet.

PETER STOLYPIN

'I must carry through effective measures of reform, and at the same time I must face the revolution, resist it and stop it.' - Pyotr Stolypin, 1906

 ## Who was Pyotr Stolypin?

Pyotr Stolypin was the Prime Minister of Russia, and Minister of Internal Affairs of the Russian Empire from 1906 to h assassination in 1911.

 ## What was Pyotr Stolypin best known for?

Stolypin was known for 6 key actions he took as prime minister:

- ☑ His policy of repression after the 1905 Revolution. Stolypin used the police and army to crush the revolutionaries.
- ☑ There were thousands of executions by hanging, or 'Stolypin's necktie', between 1906 and 1909.
- ☑ In 1906, he reformed farming by introducing a law allowing peasants to leave the commune. It also let them enclose their strips of land into small farms. Stolypin hoped this would help prevent revolution and free up labour for industrialisation.
- ☑ He introduced social reform between 1906 and 1912, including doubling spending on health, poor relief and aid for farmers.
- ☑ He introduced the Peasant Land Bank in 1906, which gave loans to peasants to buy land.
- ☑ In 1907, he changed the system for elections to the Duma *(p.36)* so only the richest third of Russia could vote. He also removed the voting rights of national minorities.

 ## What methods did Pyotr Stolypin use to keep control?

Stolypin was known for using a 'carrot and stick' approach to keep control of Russia. He introduced land and welfare reforms to appease the peasants and workers, but at the same time he violently suppressed all opposition.

 ## How successful were Pyotr Stolypin's policies?

Stolypin was successful in 5 main ways:

- ☑ Discontent was reduced. The number of political assassinations decreased from around 1200 to 385 and there were fewer peasant uprisings or strikes.
- ☑ Heavy industry increased, with a 50% growth in iron and steel production.
- ☑ Private land ownership increased, with peasants leaving the mirs.
- ☑ Working conditions in factories improved with the introduction of safety inspectors, and workers benefitted from employee insurance against accidents and sickness.

☑ His suppression of opposition worked and he was able to crush the 1905 Moscow Uprising.

How did Pyotr Stolypin's policies fail?

Stolypin failed in 5 main ways:

☑ His policies, in particular land reform, needed more time to work. He was assassinated only 5 years after it was introduced.

☑ His reforms did not go far enough to improve the living and working conditions of both the peasants and the urban workers.

☑ Discontent and opposition still existed and there were still strikes and demonstrations.

☑ His repressive measures created even more resentment.

☑ Some of his reforms were undermined by Tsar Nicholas II *(p.20)*.

What was Pyotr Stolypin's relationship with Nicholas II?

Stolypin's relationship with Tsar Nicholas II *(p.20)* changed over time:

☑ Initially, Tsar Nicholas II *(p.20)* had a positive relationship with Stolypin because he successfully suppressed uprisings in Russia.

☑ Nicholas II did undermine some of Stolypin's reforms on education and improvements in factory conditions.

☑ There is some evidence that Nicholas II was about to dismiss Stolypin as prime minister just before he was assassinated.

Why was Pyotr Stolypin important?

Pyotr Stolypin was the driving force behind reform after 1905.

How did Pyotr Stolypin die?

Stolypin was assassinated in Kiev on 18th September, 1911.

DID YOU KNOW?

3 facts about Pyotr Stolypin:

✔ When Tsar Nicholas II offered him the job of prime minister, he initially turned it down.

✔ He was assassinated in Kiev at a celebration marking the emancipation of the serfs.

✔ Some believe the Tsar was involved as the assassin was a police spy and the murder investigation was stopped.

LAND REFORM

Land reform was much needed in Russia.

What were Stolypin's land reforms?

Prime Minister Stolypin introduced a series of land reforms which tried to change the way the peasants farmed.

When did Stolypin's land reforms happen?

Stolypin introduced his agrarian (farming) reforms between 1906 and 1911.

Why were Stolypin's land reforms introduced?

There were 4 main reasons Stolypin brought in land reforms:

- ☑ To win the support of the peasants and prevent revolution by reducing support for the left.
- ☑ To modernise farming in Russia, which was incredibly backward.
- ☑ To encourage peasants to leave their communes and farm independently.
- ☑ To increase production and prosperity, which would in turn help to prevent revolution and free up labour for industrialisation. He referred to this policy as a 'wager on the strong'.

 What did Stolypin's land reforms change?

There were 3 main changes as a result of the land reforms:

- ☑ A Peasants' Land Bank was introduced to replace redemption payments, which were loans from the state. This gave loans to peasants to buy land.
- ☑ From November 1906, peasants could now leave their communes to farm their own land independently. Communes were peasant communities that owned all the land.
- ☑ There were financial incentives to move to Siberia where there was plenty of land.

 What were the results of Stolypin's land reforms?

There were 3 main consequences of the land reforms:

- ☑ By 1917, about 15% of peasants had begun farming independently.
- ☑ About 5 million peasants moved to Siberia between 1900 and 1913. However, about 750,000 came back again.
- ☑ Grain production increased by about 16 tonnes from 1906 to 1913.

 What were the problems of Stolypin's land reforms?

There were 3 key issues with the land reforms:

- ☑ Stolypin said it might take 20 years for them to be successful, but he was assassinated after only 5 years.
- ☑ Land reform was not simple. Some peasants may have left the mir (commune) but did not change the way in which they farmed. They still had strips of land scattered across the village and did not use modern methods.
- ☑ By 1917, peasant unrest increased again.

DID YOU KNOW?

Stolypin hoped the land reforms would buy the loyalty of the peasants.

He was wrong.

RUSSIFICATION

Russification was brought in as a policy in 1881 after the assassination of Tsar Alexander II.

 What was the policy of Russification?

Russification was a policy used by both Nicholas II and the communists to encourage non-Russian minorities to identify as Russian, for example by following the Russian Orthodox religion and speaking the Russian language.

Why did Nicholas II use Russification?

There were 3 main reasons why the policy of Russification was introduced:

- ✅ The different nationalities throughout Russia were difficult to manage.
- ✅ Many did not identify as Russian and their loyalty lay with their local culture and leaders instead of with Moscow.
- ✅ Some nationalities wanted independence, which was a threat.

How did Russia's leaders try to achieve Russification?

There were 10 main methods of Russification:

- ✅ Stolypin ensured that Finland became a full part of the empire in 1906.
- ✅ The Bolsheviks *(p.32)* passed the Decree on Nationalities in 1917.
- ✅ The 1918 constitution formally created the RSFSR which incorporated parts of Central Asia formally into the Empire.
- ✅ The 1924 constitution created the USSR.
- ✅ The 1936 constitution apparently gave more rights and representation to nationalities, but in reality Stalin *(p.121)* had tightened his control.
- ✅ The communists allowed nationalities to keep their own governments, but the Sovnarkom *(p.70)* always had the final say in all decisions.
- ✅ Children were taught Russian in schools.
- ✅ Restricting the practice of minority religions.
- ✅ Improving infrastructure so there were better communications between Moscow and the more distant regions of the Empire.
- ✅ Repression of uprisings and protests against the regime.

How successful was Russification?

The challenges posed by the different nationalities never went away, but there were 3 key elements of success.

- ✅ Nicholas II ensured that different nationalities were represented in the Duma *(p.36)* so that they feel more involved with the political decisions.
- ✅ Stalin *(p.121)* was able to re-incorporate areas which were lost after the Treaty of Brest-Litovsk *(p.63)*, such as Poland with the Nazi-Soviet Pact.
- ✅ The Duma *(p.36)* and constitutions, while they were in reality very limited in the freedoms they granted, placated the nationalities and prevented any mass uprisings.

How did Russification fail?

There were 5 main ways in which the policy of Russification failed:

- ✅ Minority protests contributed to the collapse of the Provisional Government *(p.50)*.
- ✅ Lenin lost huge areas of the empire with the Treaty of Brest-Litovsk *(p.63)*.
- ✅ Many nationalities failed to demonstrate true loyalty to Stalin *(p.121)*. For example, Ukrainian peasants were particularly hostile towards collectivisation.
- ✅ Many nationalities would continue with their own language and culture in secret despite the restrictions imposed.
- ✅ The different nationalities still strived for independence.

DID YOU KNOW?

The assassination of Alexander II was carried out by a group known as 'People's Will'. They wanted to overthrow the autocratic rule of the tsars.

THE LENA GOLDFIELD STRIKE, 1912

The Lena Goldfield strike and massacre had echoes of the 1905 Revolution.

What was the Lena Goldfield Massacre?

The Lena Goldfield Massacre was the killing of goldfield workers who were on strike. The workers were shot by the army. The gold fields were located by the River Lena in Siberia.

When was the Lena Goldfield Massacre?

The Lena Goldfield Massacre happened on 17th April, 1912 (or 4th April, Old Style).

What caused the Lena Goldfield strike?

The goldfield workers went on strike to protest against poor and harsh working conditions.

What did the workers demand during the Lena Goldfield strike?

The workers had 3 main demands:

- ✔ An 8-hour work day.
- ✔ An increase in wages.
- ✔ Better food; they were often given rotten meat.

What was the tsar's response to the Lena Goldfield strike?

The army and police were sent to deal with the strike:

- ✔ The administration refused to agree to the workers' demands.
- ✔ The strike committee and those on strike were arrested.
- ✔ Protestors were shot by the army, with around 270 killed and 250 injured.

What was the people's response to the Lena Goldfield strike?

The massacre sparked more strikes across the Russian Empire, with 700 being held during April 1912. According to Lenin, the Lena massacre 'inflamed the masses with revolutionary fire'.

What was the Duma's response to the Lena Goldfield strike?

The massacre was investigated by the Duma *(p.36)*. Alexander Kerensky led the investigation and reported on the terrible conditions faced by miners.

Why was the Lena Goldfield strike important?

The Lena Goldfield strike and massacre were important because they showed 2 main things:

- ✔ Working conditions for the working class were still awful.
- ✔ Nicholas II and his government would still use force to crush opposition.

DID YOU KNOW?

The government's reaction to the strike caused horror and outrage across Russia.

It was a clear signal the government had not changed and would continue to suppress all protests through harsh and lethal measures.

Quizzes, amazing exam preparation tools and more at GCSEHistory.com

RUSSIA AND THE FIRST WORLD WAR

A people's uprising.

 What happened with Russia and the First World War when it joined?

Russia joined with Britain and France in the Triple Entente, against Germany and the Triple Alliance, in the First World War.

 When did Russia enter the First World War?

Germany declared war on Russia on 1st August, 1914. Russia ended the war with Germany on 3rd March, 1918.

 Why did Russia enter the First World War?

There were 2 key reasons why Russia entered the First World War:

☑ Austria declared war on Serbia on the 28th July, 1914. Russia mobilised her troops in July to protect Serbia.

☑ Germany declared war on Russia because Russia refused to stop mobilising her troops.

 What was the public response to Russia's entry into the First World War?

There were 3 main initial responses:

☑ The people of the Russian Empire were very patriotic and supported Nicholas II.

☑ The Duma *(p.36)* and constitutions, while they were in reality very limited in the freedoms they granted, placated the nationalities and prevented any mass uprisings.

☑ The tsar *(p.19)* became more popular as the military was initially successful against Germany.

 How successful was Russia's military when they entered the First World War?

There were 3 key military defeats:

☑ Germany defeated Russia at Tannenberg in August 1914.

☑ Germany defeated Russia at Masurian Lakes in September 1914.

☑ Russia had done incredibly badly by the end of 1915. The Germans had occupied parts of Russia and 2 million men were dead or injured.

 Why did discontent grow when Russia entered the First World War?

There were 3 main reasons for growing discontent connected to the First World War:

☑ The military defeats and the German occupation.

☑ The people blamed Nicholas II and his government for the failures and the poor state of the Russian Army which had insufficient supplies.

☑ The First World War exacerbated the extreme domestic impoverishment.

 When did Tsar Nicholas II take command of Russia's army in the First World War?

Tsar Nicholas II *(p.20)* took command of the Russian army and navy in August 1915.

 Why did Tsar Nicholas II take command of Russia's war effort during the First World War?

Nicholas II thought it was his duty to take command, especially as the army had suffered several key defeats.

What were the consequences of Tsar Nicholas II taking command of Russia's war effort during the First World War?

The decision of Tsar Nicholas II *(p.20)* to assume command of the Russian Army was widely seen as a mistake for 3 key reasons:

☑ People now blamed him personally for Russia's military defeats.

☑ It caused his popularity with the people to decrease.

☑ He left Tsarina Alexandra *(p.113)* in control as regent and she was extremely unpopular.

DID YOU KNOW?

Tsar Nicholas II and Kaiser Wilhelm II were relatives.

✔ They were cousins.

✔ They sent each other telegrams in the run up to the First World War.

✔ These were called the 'Willy-Nicky' telegrams.

EFFECTS OF THE FIRST WORLD WAR

The First World War had a devastating impact on Russia.

 What were the effects of the First World War on Russia?

Russia suffered massive social, economic and political effects because of the First World War.

 What were the economic effects of the First World War on Russia?

The First World War had 5 major economic effects on Russia:

☑ The transport system could not cope because it was so archaic. There were few railways or proper roads. The whole system broke down due to the demands of the mobilisation of the army, and transporting weapons, resources and food.

☑ The number of men conscripted into the armed forces meant there was a shortage of workers in the factories and on the farms. This led to shortages of goods and food.

☑ The national debt increased because the government had to borrow money, and taxes were increased to pay for the war.

☑ Russia lost resources when Germany occupied parts of the empire. The impact of this was worsened because Germany also cut off Russia's access to their allies, on whom they relied for imports. These supplies had to come via the port of Vladivostok, which was frozen in winter.

☑ The government printed too much paper money, which caused the Russian rouble to fall in value. This led to inflation.

 What were the social effects of the First World War on Russia?

There were 4 key social effects of the First World War:

☑ Rural areas were stripped of men as they went to fight.

☑ There were food shortages because the transport system couldn't cope and food was requisitioned to feed the army.

☑ The shortages of goods and food, combined with the government printing more money, led to inflation of 200% by 1916. Working class people struggled as prices rose faster than wages.

☑ Unemployment rose in the cities. Demand for goods dropped, and factories could not get the resources they needed due to the collapse of the transport system.

What were the political effects of the First World War on Russia?

There were 5 key political effects of the First World War:

☑ There was increased opposition to Nicholas II from the fourth Duma *(p.39)*.

☑ Tsarina Alexandra *(p.113)* was made regent when Nicholas II took charge of the army. Her incompetence led to an increase in opposition to the government.

☑ There was increased criticism of the tsarina because of Rasputin's influence over her and the decisions she made.

☑ Many historians argue that Nicholas II was greatly weakened by the First World War and that his mistakes, his increased unpopularity and his defeats were the main reasons he fell from power.

☑ Others argue that Nicholas II would have fallen from power without the First World War, due to the pre-existing social and economic problems, and the political opposition he already faced. The war simply sped things up.

What were the effects of the First World War on the relationship between the tsar and the Duma in Russia?

The First World War ruined the relationship between Tsar Nicholas II *(p.20)* and the fourth Duma *(p.39)* in 4 key ways:

☑ Nicholas II initially suspended the fourth Duma *(p.39)* against its wishes in August 1914.

☑ Members criticised Nicholas II's handling of the war and demanded the Duma *(p.36)* had more of a say in how the country and the war was run. Nicholas II refused to make changes.

☑ In 1915, members of the fourth Duma *(p.39)* created the Progressive Bloc, consisting of the centre parties. It tried to make the government, and Nicholas II, more responsive to the people. It failed.

☑ The fourth Duma *(p.39)* was very critical of Tsarina Alexandra *(p.113)* and Rasputin.

What were the effects of the First World War on Tsarina Alexandra of Russia?

The First World War changed the position of Tsarina Alexandra *(p.113)* in 4 main ways:

☑ When Nicholas II took command of the army in August 1915 he made Alexandra his regent. She was now in charge in his absence.

☑ Alexandra believed in autocracy. She would not work with the fourth Duma *(p.39)* which, as a result, was very critical of her.

☑ She appointed ministers who were not always competent.

☑ She became highly criticised by the people because she was German, and because of her decisions as regent and her friendship with Rasputin.

DID YOU KNOW?

Around 15 million men served in the Russian Army during the First World War.

THE FEBRUARY (MARCH) REVOLUTION, 1917

The revolutions of 1917 were triggered by Russia's involvement in the First World War.

What was the February Revolution?

The February Revolution was the first of two revolutions which took place in Russia in 1917. The February Revolution began with strikes and riots over the lack of food.

When was the February Revolution?

The February Revolution is sometimes known as the March Revolution depending on which calendar is used. It took place between 23rd February and 3rd March, 1917, using the old calendar, or between 8th and 16th March, 1917, using the new one.

Where did the February Revolution take place?

The February Revolution of 1917 occurred in Petrograd. Petrograd, located on the Baltic Sea in the north-west of Russia, was called St Petersburg until 1914. It was then renamed, as it was felt the original name was 'too German'. It became Leningrad in 1924, after Lenin's death, and was then renamed St Petersburg once again in 1991.

What caused the February Revolution?

There were several immediate and long-term causes of the February Revolution.

What were the long-term causes of the February Revolution?

There were 4 key long-term causes:

- ✅ The discontent caused by the awful living and working conditions of the working class.
- ✅ The discontent caused by poverty and the frequent hunger suffered by peasants. There were also continuing issues with land ownership.
- ✅ Middle class anger and frustration at not having any real political power.
- ✅ The nationalities from the different provinces wanted to be independent from Russian rule.

What were the immediate causes of the February Revolution?

There were 6 key immediate causes of the February Revolution:

- ✅ The First World War caused significant disruption to Russia's economy and eroded the support for Nicholas II from the peasants, the working class, the middle class and the upper class.
- ✅ Russia was suffering from food and fuel shortages during the winter of 1916-17.
- ✅ By January 1917, the morale of the Russian Army was very low with 1.5 million deserting in 1916.
- ✅ On 9th February, there were massive strikes in Moscow and Petrograd.
- ✅ The strikes increased when, on 19th January, the Petrograd authorities announced bread would be rationed from 1st March.
- ✅ There was a huge march in Petrograd on 23rd February, celebrating International Women's Day, which became an anti-government protest against the war and the tsar. (p.19)

What were the key events of the February Revolution?

There were 6 key events during the February Revolution:

- ✅ By 25th February, 200,000 people were on strike in Petrograd.
- ✅ On 26th February, Nicholas II ordered the fourth Duma (p.39) to close down but they refused.
- ✅ On 27th February, Nicholas II ordered the army to shoot the protesters. 66,000 soldiers from the Petrograd garrison refused and mutinied, and joined the protesters instead. The Petrograd Soviet (p.49), or workers council, was created.
- ✅ On 28th February, the Petrograd Soviet (p.49) issued Order Number 1 which stated that the armed forces should only obey the orders of the Soviet. On the same day the sailors in Kronstadt mutinied. At this point, Nicholas II was asked to abdicate.
- ✅ On 1st March, the Soviets recognised the authority of the Provisional Government (p.50) set up by the fourth Duma (p.39) under the leadership of Prince Lvov (p.120).
- ✅ Tsar Nicholas II (p.20) abdicated on behalf of himself and his son on 2nd March, 1917.

What were the results of the February Revolution?

There were 3 main results of the February Revolution.

- ✅ The end of 300 years of Romanov rule and the end of the monarchy.
- ✅ This was followed by the end of the empire and the formation of the republic in th
- ✅ The establishment of dual power, or dual authority, between the Russian Provision
Petrograd Soviet *(p.49)* of Workers' and Soldiers' Deputies.

Why was the
The Petro
colla

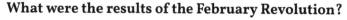 **Why did the February Revolution succeed?**

There were 6 main reasons the February Revolution succeeded:

- ✅ The main reason was the army failed to support Tsar Nicholas II *(p.20)* and refused to fire on the protesters. The mutiny meant Nicholas II could no longer rely on the support of the army to prop up his government.
- ✅ Aristocrats and key members of his own government lost faith in Nicholas II, withdrew their support, and persuaded Nicholas II to abdicate.
- ✅ There was an alternative government to Nicholas II when the fourth Duma *(p.39)* created the Provisional Government *(p.50)*, which was supported by the Petrograd Soviet *(p.49)*.
- ✅ Nicholas II was blamed for Russia's failures in the First World War and, as a result, he lost the support of many different social classes including the workers, the middle class and the aristocrats. He was left with little support.
- ✅ The shortages caused by the First World War significantly increased the amount of discontent in Russia, so opposition became much more widespread and more dangerous to Nicholas II's position.
- ✅ The reputation of the tsar's *(p.19)* government had been fundamentally weakened by the failures in the First World War and the influence Rasputin was reputed to have had over Tsarina Alexandra *(p.113)*.

DID YOU KNOW?

The February Revolution is often described as 'spontaneous' as it was not organised by a single group.

PETROGRAD SOVIET

The Petrograd Soviet played an important role in the October Revolution.

 What was the Petrograd Soviet?

The Petrograd Soviet was a council of workers' and soldiers' deputies in Russia.

 When was the Petrograd Soviet formed?

The Petrograd Soviet was formed on 12th March, 1917.

 Who was the founder of the Petrograd Soviet?

The Petrograd Soviet was formed by Leon Trotsky.

 Who were the members of the Petrograd Soviet?

The leaders of the Soviet were a mix of radical socialists, Mensheviks and Social Revolutionaries but also a small number of Bolsheviks *(p.32)*. The leadership included Trotsky and Kerensky, who was also a member of the Provisional Government *(p.50)*.

Petrograd Soviet created?

...grad Soviet was set up because of the massive unrest in Petrograd. Tsar Nicholas II's *(p.20)* government was ...sing and soldiers declared their support for the revolution.

Why was the Petrograd Soviet important?

The Petrograd Soviet was important for 4 key reasons:

- ☑ It shared power with the Provisional Government *(p.50)*, called the dual authority or dual power, between March 1917 and October 1917.

- ☑ It issued Order Number 1 on 1st March which stated the armed forces should only obey the orders of the Soviet. It should not obey the Provisional Government *(p.50)* if orders from that organisation contradicted or undermined those of the Soviet.

- ☑ It organised the defence of Petrograd during the Kornilov Revolt *(p.54)* in August 1917, using the Red Guard after the Provisional Government *(p.50)* gave them weapons.

- ☑ Trotsky used the Petrograd Soviet to help plan the October Revolution *(p.56)*.

In what ways was the Petrograd Soviet's impact limited?

The Petrograd Soviet's impact was limited in 4 key ways:

- ☑ It was reluctant to take power because there were so many problems in Russia which would be incredibly difficult to solve. They did not want to take responsibility for failing to solve these problems.

- ☑ The Mensheviks in the Petrograd Soviet believed in a socialist revolution but they did not think that Russia was ready for the revolution yet. Therefore, they wanted to fully industrialise first and have a phase where it was controlled by the bourgeoisie or upper class.

- ☑ The Petrograd Soviet was prepared to support the Provisional Government *(p.50)* because it represented the upper class and, by supporting it, the Petrograd Soviet appeared to not prioritise the needs of the workers.

- ☑ It did not want to weaken the Provisional Government *(p.50)* because they feared the tsar *(p.19)* would regain power.

DID YOU KNOW?

The idea of soviets was formed during the 1905 Revolution.

THE PROVISIONAL GOVERNMENT

The Provisional Government lost the support of the people because it made several key mistakes.

What was the Provisional Government?

The Provisional Government was the temporary government set up in Russia after Tsar Nicholas II *(p.20)* abdicated and the tsarist government collapsed.

When was the Provisional Government created?

The Provisional Government was created on 2nd March, 1917.

Who set up the Provisional Government?

The Provisional Government was created by 12 members of the fourth Duma *(p.39)*. The initial leader was Prince Lvov *(p.120)*, a liberal.

Who were the members of the Provisional Government?

The Provisional Government:

☑ Consisted of 12 members of the fourth Duma *(p.39)*.

☑ Was led by Prince Lvov *(p.120)*, a liberal, from March until July.

☑ Was led by Alexander Kerensky, a Socialist Revolutionary, from July until October.

☑ The other members were a mixture of Kadets and Octobrists.

What were the weaknesses of the Provisional Government?

The Provisional Government (PG) had 4 key weaknesses:

☑ It lacked authority because it shared power with the Petrograd Soviet *(p.49)*.

☑ It lacked legitimacy because it didn't represent the people. It was made up of mainly upper class men and was not elected by the population.

☑ It lacked power because the Petrograd Soviet's *(p.49)* Order Number One gave the Soviet control of the armed forces.

☑ It was not responsible for all areas of government because the Petrograd Soviet *(p.49)* controlled some, such as the transport system and soldiers.

What were the key actions of the Provisional Government?

The Provisional Government took 3 key actions:

☑ On 3rd March 1917, it published its eight principles of government including complete political and religious amnesty which allowed political prisoners to be released from prison, freedom of speech, and the setting up of a Constituent Assembly *(p.63)*.

☑ It published a set of decrees including an eight hour working day, minimum wage, the abolition of the death sentence and the confiscation of all Crown lands.

☑ It launched the June Offensive *(p.52)* which was unsuccessful and led to the loss of 400,000 men and mutinies. Kerensky, the Minister of War, was blamed and it led to more social unrest.

What mistakes did the Provisional Government make?

The Provisional Government made 5 key mistakes:

☑ It continued the war with Germany. It had little choice as the Allies threatened to cut off financial aid if Russia pulled out of the war.

☑ It did not successfully deal with the issue of shortages of food and goods. Its economic measures, such as an increase in income tax, were just ignored.

☑ It did not address the needs of the peasants. They wanted more land from the landlords but the Provisional Government did nothing because, in reality, it had little control over most of Russia and it would cost too much money.

☑ The Provisional Government introduced decrees which increased people's rights, including the ability to criticise its actions.

☑ It did not arrange elections, which made it seem the Provisional Government wanted to keep its power.

What are historians' opinions on the effectiveness of the Provisional Government rule Russia in 1917?

Historians debate how effectively the Provisional Government ruled Russia during its brief time in power.

How was the Provisional Government effective?

There were 4 main ways that the Provisional Government ruled Russia effectively:

☑ It appealed to the people through its liberal approach. Its key principles included freedom of speech, the release of political prisoners and the abolition of the death sentence.

☑ It passed decrees to improve working conditions including a minimum wage and an eight hour working day.

☑ It always intended to set up a Constituent Assembly *(p.63)* which would provide democratic elections.

☑ They effectively dealt with the riots and uprisings during the July Days and the Kornilov revolt *(p.54)*.

How was the Provisional Government ineffective?

There were 9 main ways the Provisional Government was ineffective in ruling Russia:

☑ It never really achieved full authority over the country because it had to share power with the Petrograd Soviet *(p.49)*.

☑ The Petrograd Soviet *(p.49)* had control of the army due to Order Number One.

☑ It was unelected and didn't really represent the people as it was mainly made up of aristocrats.

☑ It was responsible for the disastrous June Offensive *(p.52)* where 400,000 men were lost.

☑ It failed to deal with the problems of hunger and had to bring in food rationing.

☑ It was reliant on the Petrograd Soviet *(p.49)* and the Bolsheviks *(p.32)* to put down the Kornilov revolt *(p.54)*.

☑ It failed to deal with land distribution which was the main grievance for the Russian peasants.

☑ It failed to pull Russia out of the war, which meant it failed to solve many of the problems which caused the downfall of the tsar *(p.19)* in the first place.

☑ The increase in support for the Bolsheviks *(p.32)* demonstrates how unpopular the Provisional Government became. Their famous slogan, "Peace, Land, Bread", represented the key areas where the Provisional Government failed to deliver.

DID YOU KNOW?

The Provisional Government was only intended to hold power until elections could be organised for a more permanent, democratic solution.

THE JUNE OFFENSIVE, 1917

The June Offensive was the Provisional Government's major push to win the First World War. It failed.

What was the June Offensive?

The June Offensive was a Russian attack to push back the Austro-Hungarians and Germans to win the war. It was a disaster. It is also known as the July Offensive depending on which calendar you are using.

When did the June Offensive take place?

The June Offensive began on 18th June, 1917 and had collapsed by 5th July, 1917 by the old calendar. By the new calendar it began on 1st July, 1917.

Why did the June Offensive occur?

The June Offensive was launched as an attempt by Russia to achieve a crushing military victory and end the war.

Who organised the June Offensive?

As the Minister for War, it was Alexander Kerensky who organised the June Offensive.

What were the results of the June Offensive?

There were 3 key results of the June Offensive:

- ✅ Huge losses of 400,000 men. It also led to mutinies and chaos.

- ✅ Both the Provisional Government *(p.50)* and Kerensky, as the minister of war, were blamed for the failures in the war. This led to resignations, especially from the Kadets.

- ✅ The July Days were a period of social, economic and political upheaval in Russia while the Provisional Government *(p.50)* was in charge.

DID YOU KNOW?

The June Offensive is also known as the Kerensky Offensive after its leader, Alexander Kerensky.

THE JULY DAYS, 1917

The Provisional Government managed to survive the July Days and restore its reputation, but it was only a temporary reprieve.

What were the July Days in Russia?

The July Days were a period of social, economic and political upheaval in Russia while the Provisional Government *(p.50)* was in power.

When were the July Days in Russia?

The July Days happened between 3rd and 7th July, 1917.

Why did the July Days happen in Russia?

There were 3 key reasons for the July Days uprising:

- ✅ Bread rationing was brought in by the Provisional Government *(p.50)* due to shortages in March 1917. By July these food shortages had worsened.

- ✅ The June Offensive *(p.52)* had totally failed and people were war weary.

- ✅ The Bolsheviks *(p.32)*, under Lenin, had very successful anti-Provisional Government *(p.50)* propaganda.

What happened during the July Days in Russia?

There were 6 key events during the July Days uprising:

- ✅ Workers, soldiers and Kronstadt sailors protested in Petrograd.

- ✅ The Bolshevik *(p.32)* Party organised riots. The crowds used the Bolshevik slogans of 'Peace, Bread and Land', and 'All Power to the Soviets'.

- ✅ The Petrograd Soviet *(p.49)* rejected a demand for them to take control.

- ✅ The Provisional Government *(p.50)*, with the help of loyal troops, cleared the streets and regained control.

- ✅ Bolshevik *(p.32)* leaders, including Trotsky, were rounded up and 800 members were arrested and imprisoned.

- ✅ Lenin fled to Finland and the reputation of the Bolsheviks *(p.32)* was in tatters.

Who was involved with the July Days In Russia?

The protests during the July Days involved the following groups: revolutionaries, sailors, soldiers, Bolsheviks *(p.32)* and workers.

 What were the results of the July Days in Russia?

There were 3 key results of the July Days:

✅ The Provisional Government's *(p.50)* reputation was restored.

✅ The opponents of the Provisional Government *(p.50)* were imprisoned or had fled abroad, e.g. Lenin.

✅ Kerensky became the leader of the Provisional Government *(p.50)* and worked with the Kadets and Socialists.

DID YOU KNOW?

Alexander Kerensky became leader of the Provisional Government after the July Days crisis.

He was both a member of the Provisional Government and the Petrograd Soviet.

THE KORNILOV REVOLT (COUP), 1917

General Kornilov was appointed to restore discipline in the army, yet led it in a revolt.

 What was the Kornilov Revolt?

The Kornilov Revolt, or the Kornilov Coup, was an unsuccessful coup by part of the army against the Russian Provisional Government *(p.50)* and the Petrograd Soviet *(p.49)*.

 Who was the leader of the Kornilov Revolt?

General Lavr Kornilov was Commander-in-Chief of the Russian Army from July to September 1917. He was the leader of the Kornilov Revolt.

 When was the Kornilov Revolt?

It happened from 27th to 30th August, 1917, using the old calendar. (In the new calendar, 10th to 13th September, 1917).

Why did the Kornilov Revolt happen?

There are 2 main reasons why the Kornilov Revolt occurred:

✅ Prime Minister Kerensky aimed to improve army discipline so that Russia could win the First World War. He appointed General Kornilov as the commander-in-chief of the army to bring about this change.

✅ General Kornilov wanted Kerensky to declare martial law and close down the soviets. Kerensky refused and sacked Kornilov who reacted by sending troops to Petrograd.

What happened during the Kornilov Revolt?

There were 4 key events during the Kornilov Revolt:

✅ On 24th August, General Kornilov ordered troops to Petrograd to close down the Petrograd Soviet *(p.49)*.

✅ Kerensky called on the Petrograd Soviet *(p.49)* to defend the city and allowed them to arm the Red Guard and in return he freed the Bolshevik *(p.32)* prisoners arrested in the July Days uprising.

- General Kornilov's route into the city was blocked by railway workers.
- The Bolsheviks *(p.32)* stopped General Kornilov and he was arrested on 1st September, 1917.

What were the results of the Kornilov Revolt?

The Kornilov Revolt affected the government and had 5 other important consequences:

- It weakened the position of the Provisional Government *(p.50)*. They lost support from the right-wing because they had given weapons to the Bolsheviks *(p.32)*. They lost support from the left-wing because Kerensky had tried to compromise with Kornilov at first.
- The Bolsheviks *(p.32)* had more support because they had defended Petrograd from General Kornilov and now they had weapons.
- Membership of the Bolshevik *(p.32)* Party increased by about 100,000 by October.
- Because their position was strengthened, the Bolsheviks *(p.32)* were able to gain control of the Petrograd Soviet *(p.49)* by September 1917.
- Morale and discipline in the army decreased even more.

DID YOU KNOW?

General Kornilov was captured by Austrians during the First World War.

GROWTH IN SUPPORT FOR THE BOLSHEVIK PARTY

The key Bolshevik slogan was: 'Peace, Land, Bread.'

What was the Bolshevik growth in support?

There was a growth in support for the Bolshevik *(p.32)* Party between February and October 1917, during the period when the Provisional Government *(p.50)* was in charge of Russia.

When was the growth in support for the Bolsheviks?

The growth in support for the Bolsheviks *(p.32)* was between February and October 1917. In particular, there was a spurt in their growth during the summer after the Kornilov Revolt *(p.54)*.

Who supported the Bolshevik Party that led to a growth in its support?

Many soldiers, sailors and workers supported the Bolshevik *(p.32)* Party.

Why did the Bolsheviks see a growth in support?

There were 6 key reasons why support for the Bolsheviks *(p.32)* grew:

- Lenin's influence was considerable. His personality and determination encouraged other Bolsheviks *(p.32)* to follow his lead.
- Lenin's 'April Theses' promised key things to key groups. 'Peace, Land and Bread' appealed to soldiers, peasants and workers.
- People's desperation to end the First World War was a key factor in the growth of Bolshevik support.
- Bolshevik *(p.32)* newspapers spread their propaganda messages.
- The Provisional Government *(p.50)* became more unpopular after the Kornilov Revolt *(p.54)* whereas the Bolsheviks *(p.32)* became more popular as they were seen as the defenders of Petrograd.

☑ The Bolsheviks *(p.32)* were able to build the Red Guards, a private Bolshevik army, led by Leon Trotsky and arm them with the weapons given to them during the Kornilov Revolt *(p.54)*.

DID YOU KNOW?

Lenin returned to Russia from exile in April 1917, with help from the German government.

THE OCTOBER REVOLUTION, 1917

The October Revolution was led by a small dedicated group of revolutionaries.

? What was the October Revolution?

The October Revolution is sometimes called the November Revolution due to Russia using a different calendar. It was the Bolshevik-led *(p.32)* revolution to remove the Provisional Government *(p.50)* from power.

⧗ When was the October Revolution?

The October Revolution occurred on 25th and 26th October, 1917, according to the old calendar. The dates are 7th and 8th November, 1917, under the new calendar.

👤 Who led the October Revolution?

The October Revolution was organised by the Bolsheviks *(p.32)*, led by Lenin. Leon Trotsky played a major role in organising the revolution.

Why did the October Revolution happen?

There were 5 key reasons why the October Revolution occurred:

☑ There was a shift in power and popularity from the Provisional Government *(p.50)* to the Petrograd Soviet *(p.49)* after the Kornilov Revolt *(p.54)*.

☑ On 10th October, Lenin returned to Russia and was able to persuade leading Bolsheviks *(p.32)* that the party should plan for an armed uprising against the Provisional Government *(p.50)*.

☑ On 16th October, Trotsky, as the leader of the Petrograd Soviet *(p.49)*, created the Military Revolutionary Committee. This gained the support of the Peter and Paul Fortress, so the Bolsheviks *(p.32)* had the support of the military.

☑ On 24th October, the leader of the Provisional Government *(p.50)*, Kerensky, attempted to limit the power of the Bolsheviks *(p.32)* by ordering their arrest and stopping their newspapers. Trotsky used the Military Revolutionary Committee to take over key bridges and the telephone exchange.

☑ Lenin needed to act before the elections to the Constituent Assembly *(p.63)* which were scheduled for November 1917.

What happened during the October Revolution?

There were 3 key events during the actual takeover:

☑ Early in the morning of 24th-25th October, the Red Guards took control of banks, government buildings and the railway stations.

☑ In the evening of 25th October, the Red Guards entered the Winter Palace *(p.57)* and arrested the members of the Provisional Government *(p.50)* that were present.

☑ On 26th October, Lenin announced a new communist government called the Council of the People's Commissars.

Why were the Bolsheviks successful during the October Revolution?

There were 5 key reasons why the Bolsheviks *(p.32)* were successful during the October Revolution:

- ☑ Trotsky played a key role in the success of the October Revolution. He cleverly used his position as the elected leader of the Petrograd Soviet *(p.49)*, created the Military Revolutionary Committee, and helped increase support for the Bolsheviks *(p.32)*.

- ☑ The Provisional Government *(p.50)* was weak because it had lost support from all parts of society. The armed forces were crumbling because of the First World War. The peasants felt neglected as their issues had not been addressed.

- ☑ Lenin's 'April Theses' appealed to the people, was clear to understand and helped to persuade other leading Bolsheviks *(p.32)* not to support the Provisional Government *(p.50)*. His planning of the uprising was successful.

- ☑ They were funded by Germany which helped pay for their propaganda. The Germans hoped that the revolution would be successful so that Russia would pull out of the First World War.

- ☑ The Bolsheviks *(p.32)* had the support of the major industrial cities.

DID YOU KNOW?

In 1917, Lenin claimed: 'It is much easier to shout, abuse and howl than to attempt to relate, to explain.'

STORMING THE WINTER PALACE, OCTOBER 1917

The Winter Palace was used by the Provisional Government.

What was the Storming of the Winter Palace?

Members of the Red Guard and Kronstadt sailors stormed the Winter Palace. The tsars had ruled from there for centuries, and the Provisional Government *(p.50)* also ruled from the palace.

When was the Winter Palace stormed?

It took place on 25th-26th October, 1917, using the old calendar, or on 8th-9th November, 1917, using the new one.

What did the ship Aurora do to the Winter Palace?

Aurora, a cruiser harboured nearby, fired blank shots to signal the start of the attack.

What was the aftermath of the Storming of the Winter Palace?

Some members of the Provisional Government *(p.50)* were arrested when the palace was stormed, although Alexander Kerensky escaped and fled. The Bolsheviks *(p.32)* claimed they were now in power.

DID YOU KNOW?

There was no resistance to the Bolsheviks when they stormed the Winter Palace.

More people were injured in a 1920 reenactment of the storming of the Winter Palace than in the real event.

BOLSHEVIK CONSOLIDATION OF POWER

The Bolsheviks had very little control over most of Russia after the October Revolution in 1917, so had to expand it to all parts of the country.

What was the Bolshevik consolidation of power?

The Bolshevik consolidation of power was a period of time in which the Bolsheviks *(p.32)* increased their control from just Moscow and Petrograd to most of Russia.

When did the Bolshevik consolidation of power happen?

The Bolshevik consolidation of power was between 1917 and 1921.

How did the Bolsheviks consolidate their growth in power?

There were 6 main actions that the Bolsheviks *(p.32)* took to consolidate their power:

- ☑ They issued several decrees between October and December 1917, including the Decree On Peace, the Decree on Land, the Decree on Nationalities and the Decree on Workers' Rights.
- ☑ The Bolsheviks *(p.32)* shut down the Constituent Assembly *(p.63)* in January 1918.
- ☑ In March 1918, they signed the Treaty of Brest-Litovsk *(p.63)* which ended the war with Germany.
- ☑ They fought and won the civil war against the Whites and the Greens between 1918 and 1921.
- ☑ They began the Red Terror *(p.68)* by rounding up and executing thousands of their opponents.
- ☑ They brought in censorship and by 1921 had closed down all other political parties.

How did the Decree on Land help with the consolidation of the Bolsheviks' power?

The Bolsheviks *(p.32)* issued the Decree on Land in October 1917, which abolished private ownership, including land owned by the tsar *(p.19)*, the Church and private landowners. It was given to the peasants in the hope they would support the Bolsheviks.

How did the Decree on Peace help with the consolidation of Bolshevik power?

The Decree on Peace of October 1917, called for peace to be negotiated between all countries at war. Pulling Russia out of the war would mean the Bolsheviks *(p.32)* could concentrate on establishing a government and consolidating their power.

How did the Decrees on Workers' Rights help with the consolidation of Bolshevik power?

The Decrees on Workers' Rights, issued in November 1917, focused on improvements to working conditions such as pay and unemployment benefits, and put the factories under the control of the workers in the hope the workers would support them.

How did the Decree on Nationalities help with the consolidation of the Bolsheviks' growth in power?

The Decree on Nationalities issued in October 1917, stated that the different nationalities could govern themselves. This was issued in the hope that they would not use the collapse of the tsarist government to gain their independence.

How did closing the Constituent Assembly help with the consolidation of Bolshevik power?

By closing down the Constituent Assembly *(p.63)* on 6th January, 1918, Lenin prevented it being a source of opposition to the Bolsheviks *(p.32)*. He was able to ban all political parties.

DECREE ON LAND, 1917

The Land Decree was passed to win the support of the peasants.

What was the Decree on Land?

The Decree on Land nationalised all land and was issued by the Bolsheviks *(p.32)*. In other words, land was taken away from private landowners, the tsar *(p.19)*, and the Russian Orthodox Church and given to the peasants. No one was allowed to own land.

When was the Decree on Land passed?

The Decree on Land was passed in October 1917.

Who passed the Decree on Land?

The Bolsheviks *(p.32)* passed the Decree on Land.

Why was the Decree on Land issued?

The Decree on Land was passed because Lenin and the Bolsheviks *(p.32)* hoped that winning the support of the peasants would ensure a supply of food for the workers in the cities and towns.

What was the impact of the Decree on Land?

There were two main effects of the Decree on Land:

- ☑ In reality, the peasants had already been seizing land so the Decree on Land just legalised their actions.
- ☑ The land went to those who were farming it, so some of the poorer peasants, who hadn't farmed any land, were disadvantaged by the reforms.

DECREE ON PEACE, 1917

The Peace Decree would pull Russia out of the First World War.

What was the Decree on Peace?

The Decree on Peace demanded immediate peace negotiations between all countries fighting in the First World War. It stated that Russia wanted an immediate ceasefire and to start peace talks with Germany.

When was the Decree on Peace passed?

The Decree on Peace was passed in October 1917.

Who passed the Decree on Peace?

The Bolsheviks *(p.32)* passed the Decree on Peace.

Why was the Decree on Peace issued?

There were 2 main reasons why the Decree on Peace was passed:

☑ Lenin hoped communist revolutions would occur across Europe. Therefore, Germany would either be willing to negotiate a fair peace in which Russia would not lose any land nor have to pay reparations, or collapse and the negotiations would be abandoned.

☑ Lenin needed to pull out of the First World War so the Bolsheviks *(p.32)* could concentrate on gaining control of Russia.

What was the impact of the Decree on Peace?

There were 3 main effects of the Decree on Peace:

☑ The Decree on Peace led to the Bolsheviks *(p.32)* negotiating the Treaty of Brest-Litovsk *(p.63)* with Germany, which was signed on 3rd March, 1918.

☑ The Treaty involved making huge concessions to the Germans, giving them large areas of land and promising to pay them reparations.

☑ The Treaty was so hated it became one of the causes of the Russian Civil War *(p.65)*.

DID YOU KNOW?

Germany had secretly funded Lenin's return to Russia in the hope there would be a revolution and the country would withdraw from the First World War.

DECREE ON WORKERS' RIGHTS, 1917

The Workers' Decrees were passed to win the support of the workers.

What were the Decrees on Workers' Rights?

The Decrees on Workers' Rights attempted to improve working conditions for industrial workers and give them contro over the means of production instead of the business owners.

When were the Decrees on Workers' Rights passed?

The Decrees on Workers' Rights were passed in November 1917.

Who passed the Decrees on Workers' Rights?

The Bolsheviks *(p.32)* passed the Decrees on Workers' Rights.

Why were the Decrees on Workers' Rights issued?

The Bolsheviks *(p.32)* passed the Decrees on Workers' Rights to improve working conditions of the workers so they would win their support.

What did the Decrees on Workers' Rights state?

The Decrees on Workers' Rights contained 3 key decrees:

- ✅ In November 1917, the Decree on Work stated there would be an eight-hour day and a maximum 48-hour week.
- ✅ The Decree on Unemployment introduced insurance for all workers against illness, unemployment or injury.
- ✅ The Decree on Workers' Control was issued in December 1917, and handed over the running of all factories to the workers.

What were the positive impacts of the Decrees on Workers' Rights?

The positive impact of the decrees was that they gave the workers many rights they previously did not have.

What were the negative impacts of the Decrees on Workers' Rights?

There were 3 main problems with the Decrees on Workers' Rights because there was little money to support them:

- ✅ Workers gave themselves massive pay rises.
- ✅ Workers sacked or, in some cases, even killed managers.
- ✅ Production levels fell.

DID YOU KNOW?

The decree stated: 'All the laws restricting the work of factory, shop and other committees, or soviets of workers and employees, are hereby annulled."

DECREE ON NATIONALITIES, 1917

The Nationalities Decree was passed to win support of the different nationalities that made up the Russian Empire.

What was the Decree on Nationalities?

The Decree on Nationalities was a decree which promised the different nationalities within the Russian Empire that they had the right to a government of their own choice. In other words, the Bolsheviks *(p.32)* would not try to rule them.

When was the Decree on Nationalities passed?

The Decree on Nationalities was passed in October 1917.

Who passed the Decree on Nationalities?

The Decree on Nationalities was issued by the Bolsheviks *(p.32)*.

Why was the Decree on Nationalities issued?

The Decree on Nationalities was issued for two key reasons:

☑ To try to win support for the Bolshevik *(p.32)* revolution from the different ethnic minorities in the Russian Empire.

☑ It was hoped the decree would mean the different nationalities would not break away from Russian control.

DID YOU KNOW?

After the October Revolution, many regions in Russia declared independence.

✔ Ukraine declared its independence in November 1917.

✔ Finland declared its independence on 6th December, 1917.

DECLARATION OF THE RIGHTS OF THE PEOPLES OF RUSSIA,1917

The Declaration set out the rights of the people. The Bolsheviks did not uphold any of them.

 What was the Declaration of the Rights of the Peoples of Russia?

The Declaration of the Rights of the Peoples of Russia promised equality and self-determination for national minorities in an attempt to bond the various regions to the Soviet Union.

When was the Declaration of the Rights of the People signed in Russia?

The Declaration of the Rights of the Peoples of Russia was signed on 15th November, 1917.

Who signed the Declaration of the Rights of the People signed in Russia?

The Declaration of the Rights of the Peoples of Russia was signed by Lenin and Stalin *(p.121)*.

Was the Declaration of the Rights of the People in Russia ever respected?

The Soviet Union did not uphold human rights because it was a one-party dictatorship of the Communist Party. All freedoms granted were in name only - the communist government would always have the final say and there was no democratic representation.

DID YOU KNOW?

Estimates vary on the number of deaths under the communist regime.

Some historians claim up to 20 million Soviet citizens were killed by the actions of the Soviet Union.

Quizzes, amazing exam preparation tools and more at GCSEHistory.com

THE CONSTITUENT ASSEMBLY, 1918

The Constituent Assembly was to be tasked with deciding the new constitution and system of government for Russia. It was shut down on its second day.

What was the Constituent Assembly?

The Constituent Assembly was an elected body organised by the Provisional Government *(p.50)* for the purpose of establishing a new government after the collapse of the tsarist government. It would write a new constitution outlining how Russia would be governed.

When was the Constituent Assembly open?

The Constituent Assembly opened on 5th January and was closed down on 6th January, 1918.

Who closed down the Constituent Assembly?

Lenin closed the Constituent Assembly with the Red Guard. It was done at gunpoint.

Why was the Constituent Assembly closed down?

The Constituent Assembly was closed for 2 main reasons:

- ☑ The results for the Constituent Assembly were not in the Bolsheviks *(p.32)*' favour as the Socialist Revolutionaries gained 57%-58% of the vote. This meant it was not under the control of the Bolsheviks.
- ☑ The Constituent Assembly rejected a proposal from the Sovnarkom *(p.70)* which included all their decrees on land, peace and workers' rights, and a statement which gave all power to the Soviets.

What were the election results for the Constituent Assembly?

The results for the Constituent Assembly are disputed because the elections were interrupted and not all votes were returned. Socialist Revolutionaries won 57-58% of the vote, the Bolsheviks *(p.32)* won 25%, the Kadets won 5% and the Mensheviks won 3%.

DID YOU KNOW?

Lenin closed down the Constituent Assembly at gunpoint, claiming it was elected on an electoral register that did not fully represent the people.

THE TREATY OF BREST-LITOVSK, MARCH 1918

Lenin described the Treaty of Brest-Litovsk as: 'That abyss of defeat, dismemberment, enslavement and humiliation.'

What was the Brest-Litovsk Peace Treaty?

The Treaty of Brest-Litovsk ended Russia's role in the First World War. The treaty was signed at German-controlled Brest-Litovsk after two months of negotiations.

When was the Brest-Litovsk treaty signed?

The Treaty of Brest-Litovsk was signed on 3rd March, 1918.

Who signed the Brest-Litovsk Treaty?

The treaty was between the new Bolshevik *(p.32)* government of Russia and the Central Powers - the German Empire, Austria-Hungary, Bulgaria and the Ottoman Empire.

Where was the Brest-Litovsk Treaty signed?

The Treaty of Brest-Litovsk was signed at the German Army's headquarters in Brest-Litovsk, which at that time was part of Poland. It is in modern Belarus.

Why did the Bolsheviks agree to sign the Brest-Litovsk Treaty?

There were 6 main reasons why the Bolsheviks *(p.32)* agreed to sign the treaty:

- ☑ They had staked everything, and won all their support, on the promise of immediate withdrawal from the war.
- ☑ The Bolsheviks *(p.32)* agreed to sign because they needed a swift end to war; Russia was not able to defeat Germany.
- ☑ If Russia lost the war, it would mean the end of the Bolshevik *(p.32)* revolution.
- ☑ They believed Germany and the rest of Europe would also have communist revolutions, which would result in the treaty being overturned.
- ☑ Their priority was dealing with opposition to the Bolshevik *(p.32)* revolution inside Russia, and they feared a civil war would begin.
- ☑ They could not afford to fight Germany and a civil war at the same time.

What was the outcome of the Brest-Litovsk Treaty?

There were 3 main terms of the treaty.

- ☑ Russia lost Finland, Estonia, Latvia, Lithuania, Ukraine, Georgia, and parts of Poland from its empire - this was more than a quarter of its farmland and railroads.
- ☑ It lost 26% of its population, or 62 million people.
- ☑ Germany imposed reparations, or compensation, of 300 million roubles.

What was the impact of the Treaty of Brest-Litovsk on Russia and the Bolshevik Party?

There were 4 main effects of the Treaty of Brest-Litovsk on Russia and the Bolshevik *(p.32)* Party:

- ☑ It was considered a humiliation so people were furious with the Bolshevik *(p.32)* Party for signing it.
- ☑ The land that Russia lost to Germany was some of the best farmland it had, so food shortages worsened.
- ☑ This led to mass migration of people from the towns and cities to the countryside in the search for food.
- ☑ Many right-wing people and tsarists were so horrified by the treaty that they were even more determined to oppose the Bolsheviks *(p.32)*. This led to the civil war.

DID YOU KNOW?

The Russian delegates were told to drag out the peace negotiations.

Lenin hoped communist revolutions would spread across Europe, leading to the end of the First World War. He instructed the Russian delegates to draw out peace negotiations with the Germans. It wasn't until the Germans restarted fighting on the Eastern Front that the Russians signed the treaty.

Quizzes, amazing exam preparation tools and more at GCSEHistory.com

THE COMMUNIST PARTY, 1918

The Bolsheviks changed their name to the Russian Communist Party.

? What was the Communist Party?

Soon after seizing power in Petrograd in November 1917, the Bolsheviks *(p.32)* began to refer to themselves as communists.

⌛ When did the Bolsheviks became the Communist Party?

The Russian Communist Party was named in March 1918.

★ What did the Communist Party believe in?

The Communist Party held 3 main beliefs:

- ☑ The theory of communism of Karl Marx.
- ☑ This theory stated that there would be a revolution in which the workers would rise up and abolish the private ownership of land, property and business.
- ☑ Power would be in the hands of the workers and would be run for the benefit of the workers.

DID YOU KNOW?

The Communist Party of the Soviet Union was in power until 1991.

THE CIVIL WAR, 1918-1921

The Bolsheviks' victory in the Russian Civil War centralised their control of both the country and their own party.

? What was the Russian Civil War?

A civil war was triggered by opposition to the Bolsheviks *(p.32)* from various groups, including monarchists who wanted the tsar *(p.19)* back in power, anti-communists, groups angered by Brest-Litovsk and different nationalities who wanted their independence.

⌛ When was the Russian Civil War?

The Russian Civil War took place from 1918 to 1921.

👤 Who fought in the Russian Civil War?

The Russian Civil War was fought between communist (Red) and anti-communist (White) forces. In addition, a number of countries, including Britain and the USA, sent troops to support the Whites. The Reds won.

★ What were the different armies involved in the Russian Civil War?

There were 3 main groups involved:

- ☑ The Red Army, who were the Bolsheviks *(p.32)* or communists.
- ☑ The White Army, made up of nationalists and monarchists.
- ☑ The Green Army was formed by the peasants.

What were the causes of the Russian Civil War?

There were 5 key reasons why the Russian Civil War happened:

☑ The Russian Empire had collapsed because many nationalities wanted independence and the Bolshevik *(p.32)* Decree on Nationalities allowed this. People who were pro-Empire wanted to re-conquer these areas.

☑ Political opposition had grown towards the Bolsheviks *(p.32)* from the Social Revolutionaries, the Mensheviks, the Constituent Assembly *(p.63)*, and the anti-Bolshevik alliance to form the Whites. People objected to the fact the Bolsheviks had seized power undemocratically.

☑ The Allies were opposed to the Bolsheviks *(p.32)* pulling out of the First World War and the signing of the Treaty of Brest-Litovsk *(p.63)*. They hoped that by supporting the Whites, the Bolsheviks would be defeated and Russia would re-enter the war.

☑ Law and order had broken down.

☑ Food requisitioning by the Bolsheviks *(p.32)* angered the peasants and so they formed the Green Army to defend their homes.

 What were the consequences of the Russian Civil War on international relations?

The Russian Civil War had 3 main consequences for international relations:

☑ It increased the Soviet Union's suspicion that the capitalist West would always seek to overthrow communism.

☑ In order to protect the USSR from future foreign interference, Lenin, the leader of the USSR, pursued a policy of worldwide communist revolution.

☑ This in turn caused a 'Red Scare' in 1920s America as many feared the worldwide spread of communism.

 Who fought against the Bolsheviks in the Russian Civil War?

There were 3 main groups that opposed the Bolsheviks *(p.32)*:

☑ The Whites consisted of lots of different groups such as Socialist Revolutionaries, tsarists/monarchists, Liberals, ultra-conservatives, and army officers against the Treaty of Brest-Litovsk *(p.63)*.

☑ The Greens consisted of peasants and deserters from other armies.

☑ Foreign countries also intervened in the civil war against the Bolsheviks *(p.32)*. Britain, Japan and USA all interfered.

 What were the key events of the Russian Civil war?

There were 9 key events during the Russian Civil War:

☑ Trotsky became the Commissar for War for the Bolsheviks *(p.32)* and took charge of the Red Army on 13th March, 1918.

☑ In May 1918, the Czech Legion rebelled against the Red Army. They were leaving Russia when Trotsky demanded their weapons. They responded by allying with the Socialist Revolutionaries and taking over parts of the Trans-Siberian Railway.

☑ On 17th July, 1918, Tsar Nicholas II *(p.20)* and his family were executed in Yekaterinburg to prevent the Whites and the Czech Legion from rescuing them and using them as a rallying point in the Civil War.

☑ In August 1918, Trotsky increased the harsh discipline in the Red Army so that one in every ten soldiers was shot if he retreated.

☑ The Bolsheviks *(p.32)* suffered a major set-back during the Eastern Front Offensive led by one of the White's leaders, Admiral Kolchak. He attacked in June 1918. However, the Red Army managed to force the Whites to retreat by June 1919.

☑ By October 1919, the Red Army had managed to stop General Yudenich's advance on Petrograd and General Denikin's advance on Moscow.

☑ Between April and October 1920, the Bolsheviks *(p.32)* were also at war with Poland until they signed the Treaty of Riga in October.

☑ The Whites were finally defeated at the Battle of Perekop between 7th and 15th November, 1920.

☑ In 1921, the Green Army, led by General Makhno, was finally defeated in the Ukraine and by Tambov where about 50,000 peasants had led an uprising against the Bolsheviks *(p.32)*.

Why did the Bolsheviks win the Russian Civil War?

There are 6 main reasons why the Bolsheviks *(p.32)* won:

☑ The Bolsheviks *(p.32)* had control of the industrial heartlands and transport links, which gave them a great advantage over their enemies. They had control over factories which made munitions.

☑ The Bolsheviks *(p.32)* had a strong, well-organised propaganda machine and used art, posters and entertainment to spread their message.

☑ They introduced conscription into the Red Army so they had five million soldiers by 1921.

☑ As commissar for war, Trotsky introduced harsh military discipline, recruited tsarist officers for their experience and used the agitprop trains to spread propaganda. He turned the Red Army into an effective force and his harsh discipline ensured loyalty to the Reds.

☑ The Red Terror *(p.68)* undermined opposition to the Bolsheviks *(p.32)* as the Cheka *(p.89)*, or secret police, executed 50,000 of their enemies in 1918 including the tsar *(p.19)* and his family.

☑ Lenin's economic policy of War Communism took control of food production and manufacturing, which ensured the army was supplied.

Why did the Whites lose the Russian Civil War?

There were 6 key reasons why the Whites lost the civil war:

☑ They were reliant on foreign assistance for supplies and money, so the Whites were portrayed as the invading army.

☑ There was a severe lack of planning because they did not have one single leader as it was not a unified group.

☑ There were problems with communication, geographical distances and rivalry between the leaders.

☑ They were not united by a single goal as some wanted a return to tsarism, others favoured a military dictatorship and others preferred the Constituent Assembly *(p.63)*.

☑ The Whites did not control the major areas of industry, population or transport links because they tended to be on the outer edges of Russia.

☑ As a result their army was smaller and not as well supplied.

What were the consequences of the Russian Civil War?

There were 5 main consequences of the civil war.

☑ The Bolsheviks consolidated *(p.58)* their control over the country, economically with the policy of War Communism and politically as they destroyed their opposition using the Red Terror *(p.68)* and by winning the civil war.

☑ The policy of War Communism left the country economically ruined as food production and manufacturing collapsed.

☑ There was unrest with strikes and several different peasant uprisings, including the Tambov Uprising from 1920 to 1921, and the Kronstadt Uprising in 1921.

☑ Around eight million people died.

☑ The leaders of the Bolshevik *(p.32)* Party centralised control over their party as well as the country. All decisions were made by seven to nine key members of the Politburo *(p.71)* and orders were passed down to the rank and file.

DID YOU KNOW?

Power was centralised in the Politburo, the key decision-making body of the Communist Party.

THE RED TERROR

...Red Terror was a vicious attack on the Bolsheviks' opponents.

...led *(p.32)* repression of their opposition during the Russian Civil War *(p.65)*.

...Russia happen?

...om September 1918 to 1920.

Who carried out the Red Terror?

The Red Terror was implemented by the Cheka *(p.89)*, the Bolshevik *(p.32)* secret police force, led by Felix Dzerzhinsky.

Why was the Red Terror carried out?

There were 2 main reasons why the Red Terror happened:

- ☑ On 30th August 1918, Fanya Kaplan, a Socialist Revolutionary, attempted to assassinate Lenin because he shut down the Constituent Assembly *(p.63)* in January 1918.
- ☑ There was an attempted rebellion by the Socialist Revolutionaries in Moscow in July 1918.

What happened during the Red Terror?

The Red Terror involved 4 key events:

- ☑ Identifying, rounding up and arresting anyone suspected of 'counter-revolutionary' activities. In other words, anyone who was a threat to the Bolshevik *(p.32)* Party.
- ☑ The existing law courts were replaced by Revolutionary Tribunals. Officially, these were established to help the struggle against counter-revolutionary forces and defend the revolution.
- ☑ It is estimated that between 200,000 and 400,000 people died because of the Red Terror between 1918 and 1920.
- ☑ The party could force anyone to do hard labour and could execute anyone who resisted.

How did the Red Terror help the Bolsheviks win the Civil War?

The Red Terror helped the Bolsheviks *(p.32)* win the civil war in 4 main ways:

- ☑ It led to the execution of Tsar Nicholas II *(p.20)* and his family which removed the threat of the monarchy being restored to power.
- ☑ It removed many who opposed the Bolsheviks *(p.32)* and therefore weakened the opposition as a whole.
- ☑ It created fear and terror, which discouraged opposition.
- ☑ It was used to force the peasants to hand over grain during requisitioning, which ensured the Red Army was fed.

How many died during the Red Terror in Russia?

It's estimated that between 200,000 and 400,000 people were executed during the Red Terror between 1918 and 1920. Prison camps were also established on the Solovetsky Islands.

DID YOU KNOW?

The terror tactics used by the Cheka were extreme. There were stories of people having their hands placed in boiling water.

Quizzes, amazing exam preparation tools and more at GCSEHistory.com

THE KRONSTADT MUTINY, 1921

The Kronstadt Mutiny was a serious concern for Lenin as previously loyal sailors turned against the Communist Party.

What was the Kronstadt Naval Mutiny?

The Kronstadt Naval Mutiny, or the Kronstadt Uprising, was a revolt by sailors at the Kronstadt Naval base against the Bolsheviks *(p.32)* which was crushed by the Red Army.

When was the Kronstadt Naval Mutiny?

The Kronstadt Naval Mutiny happened between 28th February and 16th March, 1921.

Who was involved in the Kronstadt Naval Mutiny?

The sailors from the Kronstadt Naval base. Initially, sailors on the battleship Petropavlovsk mutinied. This spread to the whole naval base and about 15,000 sailors were involved.

What did the sailors demand in the Kronstadt Naval Mutiny?

The sailors made 4 key demands:

- ☑ New elections.
- ☑ Freedom of speech.
- ☑ Equal rations.
- ☑ The scrapping of the militia units which were taking grain from the peasants.

Why did the Kronstadt Naval Mutiny happen?

There were 6 main reasons why the Kronstadt Mutiny happened:

- ☑ War Communism was causing terrible suffering. The Bolsheviks *(p.32)* cut the bread ration by a third on 22nd January, 1921.
- ☑ On 23rd February, the Mensheviks and Social Revolutionaries organised a strike supported by workers from the local factories and shipyards.
- ☑ The Kronstadt sailors hated how Bolshevik *(p.32)* party leaders got special privileges, such as extra food.
- ☑ They objected to the Red Terror *(p.68)* as people were being arrested and executed without a fair trial.
- ☑ So, on 28th February, the crew of the ship Petropavlovsk mutinied because they felt the Bolsheviks *(p.32)* had drifted away from true communism.
- ☑ They wanted 'equal rations for all the working people' and 'freedom for the peasants'.

What happened during the Kronstadt Naval Mutiny?

There were 3 important events during the Kronstadt Naval Mutiny:

- ☑ The sailors on the battleship Petropavlovsk mutinied on 28th February, 1921.
- ☑ The sailors wrote a 15 point petition which included the demand for free elections to the soviets, equal rations and freedom of the press.
- ☑ There was a mass meeting of 15,000 sailors to discuss their demands and they adopted the slogan 'All power to the soviets - not to parties'.

What was the Bolsheviks response to the Kronstadt Naval Mutiny?

Lenin and the Bolsheviks *(p.32)* responded in 3 key ways:

- ☑ Initially, Lenin issued an ultimatum ordering the sailors to surrender, which they ignored.

- ✅ Trotsky organised attacks on the Kronstadt Naval base using 50,000 troops from Red Army and artillery. The Cheka *(p.89)* were placed behind the Red Army troops and they shot any soldiers who retreated or refused to fire on the sailors.
- ✅ The Red Army had crushed the Kronstadt Mutiny by 17th March, 1921.

What were the results of the Kronstadt Naval Mutiny?

There were 5 key results of the Kronstadt Naval Mutiny:

- ✅ 10,000 Red Army soldiers were killed. 500 sailors were shot immediately and a further 2,000 were executed.
- ✅ About 4,000 were sent to Siberia to the gulags (labour camps) and about 8,000 fled to Finland.
- ✅ Lenin was very worried that previously loyal sailors had mutinied.
- ✅ As a result, he realised he needed to change his economic policy. He ended War Communism and brought in the New Economic Policy (NEP *(p.73)*).
- ✅ In March 1921, Lenin banned factions at the 10th Party Congress. He issued a decree, 'On Party Unity' which stated that factions were not allowed in the party - everyone had to support the policies of the party or they would be expelled from the party.

DID YOU KNOW?

The leader of the rebellion, Stepan Petrichenko, fled to Finland afterwards.

THE SOVNARKOM

The Sovnarkom was the cabinet of the Communist government.

What was the Sovnarkom?

The Sovnarkom was the Council of People's Commissars, also known as the SVK. It was established after the October Revolution *(p.56)* and focused on creating the USSR. It was the cabinet of the communist government made up of 13 to 20 People's Commissars. It issued the Bolsheviks *(p.32)* decrees.

Who was the leader of the Sovnarkom?

Lenin was the first chairman of the Sovnarkom.

When was the Sovnarkom formed?

The first Sovnarkom was created after the 1917 October Revolution *(p.56)*. When the Soviet Union was established, the Sovnarkom evolved to become its greatest executive or law-making authority.

How were the members of the Sovnarkom selected?

The members of the Sovnarkom were elected by the Central Executive Committee, which oversaw the work of the government. In reality, it consisted of the Communist Party's most powerful leaders from its central committee. In other words, the Sovnarkom was controlled by the Communist Party.

DID YOU KNOW?

The Sovnarkom met almost every day during the Russian Civil War

---

THE POLITBURO

The Politburo was the most important body of the Communist Party.

? What was the Politburo?

The Politburo was part of the Communist Party of Russia and subsequently the Soviet Union. It consisted of 7 to 9 main members of the party. It was the highest policy-making authority in the party; they made all of the decisions.

⧖ When was the Politburo formed?

The Politburo was created in October 1917. From 1952 to 1966, it was renamed the Presidium.

● Who were the first members of the Politburo?

Lev Kamenev, Vladimir Lenin, Joseph Stalin *(p.121)*, Leon Trotsky and Grigory Zinoviev were the first members of the Politburo.

★ What was the power of the Politburo?

The Politburo was the most powerful body in the whole of the USSR. Its members made all key policy decisions, passing them to the other sections of the Communist Party and to the government through the Sovnarkom *(p.70)*.

★ How did Lenin use the Politburo?

Lenin used the Politburo to run the country. He did allow some debate and difference of opinion. During the Civil War, it took over decision-making from the central committee.

★ How did Stalin use the Politburo?

Under Stalin *(p.121)* the Politburo lost its role as the central decision-making authority as he established a personalised dictatorship.

DID YOU KNOW?

Arkady Shevchenko, a Soviet diplomat famous for his defection to the USA, described Politburo meetings as 'quiet, orderly, and methodical'.

WAR COMMUNISM, 1918-1921

War communism helped the Bolsheviks win the civil war because it gave them full control over the population. It ensured the army was well fed and had necessary supplies.

? What was War Communism?

War Communism was an economic policy of the Bolsheviks *(p.32)* in which the state took control of the means of production, eg all factories, transport and farming. The government decided what was produced, when and by whom, and who would receive the goods.

⧖ When was War Communism introduced?

War Communism was introduced in June 1918 and ended in March 1921.

Who introduced War Communism?

Lenin and the Bolsheviks *(p.32)* introduced the policy of War Communism.

Why was War Communism introduced?

There were 4 important reasons why War Communism was brought in:

- ✅ The economy had collapsed due to the disruption caused by the First World War and the civil war, and the Bolsheviks *(p.32)* needed a way to deal with the shortages of food and goods.
- ✅ War Communism as a policy seemed to fit the communist theory as no one individual made a profit from their labour, the state controlled the means of production (the factories), and the state distributed produce according to the needs of the individual.
- ✅ The peasants were seen as resisting the Bolsheviks *(p.32)* by not supplying enough food for the cities, towns and the Red Army.
- ✅ The policy would ensure that the Red Army was supplied to fight in the civil war.

What were the aims of War Communism?

There were 3 key aims of the policy of War Communism:

- ✅ To gain control of the economy to enable them to win the war.
- ✅ To ensure enough supplies to resource the Red Army.
- ✅ To increase the Communist Party's control of the country.

What were the key features of War Communism?

There were 5 key features of War Communism:

- ✅ All industries were nationalised under the control of the Supreme Council of the Economy, or Vesenkha, in December 1917. Factories were set production targets.
- ✅ Military-style discipline was brought into the factories, which meant strikes were banned and there were harsh labour laws.
- ✅ Food rationing was introduced. Soldiers got the most, then workers, while the bourgeois and clergy received the least.
- ✅ Forced requisitioning of agricultural produce by 150,000 Bolsheviks *(p.32)*. There was strict price controls on all agricultural produce.
- ✅ All private trade was banned.

What were the positive effects of War Communism?

There were 2 important positive results of War Communism for the Bolshevik *(p.32)* Party:

- ✅ They were able to supply and feed the Red Army during the civil war which helped them to defeat the Whites and the Greens.
- ✅ They were able to centralise their control of the economy.

What were the negative effects of War Communism?

There were 7 important negative economic and social results of War Communism:

- ✅ Production levels collapsed even more. For example, coal production was 29 million tons in 1913 but by 1921 it was only 9 million.
- ✅ Food production collapsed to 48% of the 1913 productions levels. In 1913, 80 million tons of grain had been produced but in 1921, it was 37.6 million.
- ✅ There was an increase in violence and unrest in the countryside as peasants resisted food requisitioning. They hid their grain and slaughtered their animals rather than handing them over to the Bolsheviks *(p.32)*.
- ✅ By 1921, some regions faced famine. 29 million experienced famine and 5 million died.

- ☑ Workers from the cities and towns migrated to the countryside in search of food because there was less food in the towns.
- ☑ It resulted in peasant uprisings in 1920 and 1921, including the Tambov Uprising, and the Kronstadt Uprising by sailors in March 1921.
- ☑ A black market developed because of the shortages in goods and food.

DID YOU KNOW?

In many ways, war communism was an early version of a command economy.

The policy extended the Communist Party's control to all parts of the economy so it could direct resources where it wanted them.

NEW ECONOMIC POLICY, 1921-1928

The New Economic Policy was a retreat from the government holding complete control of the economy.

What was the NEP?

The New Economic Policy (NEP) was the Soviet government's economic policy. It represented a temporary retreat from its previous policy of War Communism.

When was the NEP introduced?

The New Economic Policy was introduced in 1921 and lasted until 1928.

Why was the NEP introduced?

There were 4 key reasons why the NEP was introduced:

- ☑ The previous economic policy of War Communism had resulted in economic collapse and famine in some areas of the USSR.
- ☑ War Communism had also resulted in massive unrest among the workers and the number of strikes increased.
- ☑ The peasants had risen up in protest against War Communism with one of the most serious revolts in Tambov, requiring 50,000 Red Army soldiers to crush it.
- ☑ The Kronstadt Mutiny in March 1921, by the sailors in the Kronstadt Naval base made the Bolsheviks *(p.32)* realise the dangers of continuing with the policy of War Communism.

How did the NEP work?

The NEP worked with 5 key features:

- ☑ Private ownership of businesses or banks that employed less than 20 people was allowed.
- ☑ Grain requisitioning from the peasants was stopped. Instead, they could sell it, keep the money and pay tax on anything they sold at a rate of 10%.
- ☑ The government kept control of heavy industry (coal, electricity, metal etc) and any large businesses.
- ☑ Money was reintroduced and so were some other aspects of the free market.
- ☑ People now had to pay taxes, first in goods and later in cash.

Who were the opponents of the NEP?

Some communists were disappointed with the NEP. They opposed it because they felt it betrayed their communist principles. Trotsky was one of those who opposed the NEP.

 What were the positive effects of the NEP?

There were 5 key positive effects of the NEP:

☑ Grain production had increased by 50% by 1923.

☑ In 1922 the government introduced a new currency, called chervonets, which helped to stabilise the value of money.

☑ The prices of factory-made goods increased and there was greater demand for manufactured goods, especially from the countryside.

☑ There were fewer strikes and less discontent in the countryside.

☑ Trade with foreign countries increased, which helped the USSR financially.

 What were the negative effects of the NEP?

There were 7 main negative effects of the NEP:

☑ Trade with other countries remained lower than that of 1913.

☑ Inequality also increased as some private business owners became richer. These were called NEPmen.

☑ Grain production increased, but it still wasn't enough to export large enough quantities abroad to get enough hard currency to fund industrialisation.

☑ Agriculture was still incredibly backwards.

☑ In 1923, there was the 'Scissors Crisis'. This was when food prices fell due to the supply of food increasing. However, the price of manufactured goods increased due to a shortage of manufactured goods. This made it difficult for peasants, who were earning less, and struggling to buy manufactured goods.

☑ Due to the Scissors Crisis the government forced the peasants to cut food prices. The peasants responded by feeding grain to their animals as meat was more expensive, meaning they made more money. By 1927, the amount of grain the government received decreased.

☑ Politically, Lenin came up against a lot of criticism as he was seen to have moved away from communist principles.

 How did the NEP affect women?

In general, women's economic position worsened in 3 key ways as a result of the NEP.

☑ They were forced to give up their jobs for demobilised soldiers.

☑ The government did not see women's rights as a priority, and investment in the service industries was reduced.

☑ Following the revolution, gender equality only improved slightly.

 Why was there opposition to the NEP?

There were 4 main reasons why different groups opposed the NEP:

☑ Some Bolsheviks *(p.32)* saw the NEP as a return to capitalism because it allowed people and small, privately owned businesses to make a profit. This was not acceptable to them and they believed the policy of War Communism was more aligned to their beliefs.

☑ The workers still suffered because of the increase in food prices, while unemployment increased and real wages only passed the 1914 level by 1928. In reality, workers were struggling to afford basic necessities.

☑ Some peasants were getting richer and there was growing inequality between the richer peasants called 'Kulaks' and ordinary peasants.

☑ Women were hit particularly hard as many were forced out of their jobs when the Red Army demobilised after the civil war and they ended up on the streets.

COMMUNIST POLICIES ON WOMEN, 1917-1941

All people are deemed equal in communism. In reality, women never obtained equality with men.

What was the communist view on women?

According to the theory of communism, all people are equal. Therefore, women should be treated equally to men. The Communist Party introduced a considerable amount of legislation to significantly improve women's rights; however, there were limitations in changing cultural attitudes and sexism still existed.

What policies did the communists bring in to improve the legal rights of women?

After the October Revolution *(p.56)* of 1917, the communists brought in 4 key policies to improve women's legal rights:

- ☑ 1917: Women and men were declared equal, women were given the right to vote and divorce was made easier.
- ☑ 1919: The Zhenotdel, a section of the Communist Party devoted to women's affairs headed by Alexandra Kollontai, was set up to improve their rights and position.
- ☑ 1920: Abortion was legalised.
- ☑ 1926: Women were able to own property separately from their husbands.

What policies did the communists bring in to improve the education of women?

After the October Revolution *(p.56)* of 1917, the communists brought in 3 main policies to improve education opportunities for women:

- ☑ In 1918, the Soviet Government issued a decree on education in which school was made compulsory for all children aged eight to 17.
- ☑ In 1929, 20% of higher education places were reserved for women.
- ☑ By 1940, over 40% of engineering students were women.

What policies did the communists bring in to improve work for women?

After the October Revolution *(p.56)* of 1917, the communists brought in 4 main policies to improve career opportunities for women:

- ☑ The law was changed to state men and women should be paid the same.
- ☑ Between 1918 and 1921, women were conscripted to work during the civil war to replace male workers.
- ☑ In 1923, Alexandra Kollontai became the world's first female ambassador, serving in Norway.
- ☑ By 1928, there were three million women workers. Stalin's *(p.121)* Five Year Plans and the rapid industrialisation of the USSR increased the number of women workers to over 13 million by 1940.

What were the positive results for women because of communist policies?

There were 4 important positive results for women because of the policies introduced by the communist government:

- ☑ The legal changes did greatly improve the status of women, specifically for women in predominantly Muslim republics such as Azerbaijan.

- ☑ There were massive increases in the number of female workers during the civil war so there were greater job opportunities.
- ☑ Women were working in professions they had not been able to access before.
- ☑ Women were playing a greater role in politics and a few, but not many, did reach the higher levels of government.

 What were the limitations of communist policies for women?

Despite the communist government's policies for women, there were still 10 significant limitations:

- ☑ Changing their legal status did not change society's traditionally sexist views, meaning many women faced a double burden of working and completing all household tasks.
- ☑ In reality, women did not see equality in the workplace. They did not get promoted, faced sexism and only received about 2/3 of a man's wage.
- ☑ Some communist policies had a negative impact on women. For example, making divorce easier made many women's lives worse as 70% of divorces were initiated by men. Often a pregnant wife would be abandoned, leaving them as a single parent with no financial support.
- ☑ There were negative reactions to some communist policies. For example, the campaign for the unveiling of Muslim women led to violence and honour killings.
- ☑ There were still only a few women in important roles in the government, and in 1930 only 15% of the party membership were women.
- ☑ The Zhenotdel was closed down in 1930 as the communist government claimed equality had been achieved.
- ☑ Stalin's *(p.121)* Great Retreat *(p.111)* of 1936 meant there was a return to traditional family values. Under the 1936 Family Code, abortion was made illegal and divorce became more expensive.
- ☑ Stalin's *(p.121)* collectivisation policy had a terrible impact on women in the countryside as men migrated to towns and cities in search of work.
- ☑ Women in the countryside faced lower pay, lower standards of living and fewer services.
- ☑ By the 1950s, there was an imbalance between the genders in the countryside as the number of women vastly outnumbered men. This was largely due to the number of soldiers who had died in the Second World War.

DID YOU KNOW?

In 1925, Stalin proclaimed: 'Nnot a single great movement of the oppressed... has been able to do without the participation of working women.'

COMMUNIST POLICIES ON EDUCATION, 1917-1941

The communists inherited a country whose people could barely read or write.

 What was the communist view on education?

Education was important to the communists as a way to create a new, loyal generation with the right values. They wanted to create new 'Soviet men' and 'Soviet women'.

 What were the problems in the education system that the communists had to deal with?

There were 5 important problems the communists faced in education with the system they inherited from the tsarist regime:

- ☑ Many children did not attend school as they had to pay and could not afford it.
- ☑ There were not enough schools or teachers.

- ☑ Many schools were run by the Russian Orthodox Church and the communists were atheists; they did not believe in God.
- ☑ There was a lack of resources and supplies for schools as they were underfunded.
- ☑ There were very high levels of illiteracy. Approximately 65 million people were illiterate, and only 32% of the population could read and write in 1914.

 ## What education policies did the Communist Party introduce?

The communists brought in 6 main policies over time:

- ☑ A Commissariat of Education was set up in 1917. It promised free and compulsory education for all children aged seven to 17 and the expansion of university education.
- ☑ In 1918, the Soviet government issued a decree on education which nationalised all religious schools, banned corporal punishment, homework and exams, and established unified labour schools so that children aged seven to 17 received training for work.
- ☑ In 1919, the campaign for the 'liquidation of illiteracy' was introduced to end illiteracy. Rabfaki, or remedial schools, were set up to teach basic literacy and numeracy. All soldiers in the Red Army had to attend literacy classes.
- ☑ In 1929, the government introduced a quota system for working class students entry into university. This was to encourage working class students to attend.
- ☑ In 1930, Stalin *(p.121)* focused again on eliminating illiteracy and made primary school compulsory for all children up to the age of 12.
- ☑ In 1936, Stalin *(p.121)* reversed some of the early communist education policies because of the problems they created. In his Great Retreat *(p.111)*, he re-introduced traditional teaching methods and discipline, subjects and textbooks set by the government.

 ## How did Stalin control education in communist Russia?

There were 6 main ways in which Stalin *(p.121)* controlled education:

- ☑ In the Great Retreat *(p.111)* of the 1930s, he introduced stricter controls in education.
- ☑ The government provided official textbooks which had to be used. One example was 'The Short Course of the History of the All Union Communist Party' which glorified Stalin's *(p.121)* role in the revolution.
- ☑ The government controlled the curriculum and subjects such as Russian, communist ideology and science were made compulsory.
- ☑ There was very strict teacher discipline and students had to wear uniforms and sit in rows.
- ☑ All children had to attend school until the age of 15.
- ☑ Students were indoctrinated with socialist views at school and through the youth group, the Pioneers.

 ## What were the results of the communist education policies?

There were 6 key effects of the communists' education policies:

- ☑ The initial changes of 1919 created problems as schools lacked discipline.
- ☑ Many children did not attend, especially in the countryside, or disappeared at harvest time.
- ☑ Schools were underfunded during the civil war and New Economic Policy period, and schools still charged fees.
- ☑ By 1928, about 60% of primary aged children were in school. By 1932, that had increased to 95%.
- ☑ The literacy drive was incredibly successful as 90% of Soviet adults attended a course. By 1939, over 94% of the population was literate.
- ☑ The policy of collectivisation and Stalin's *(p.121)* purges had a negative effect on education as teachers were attacked and removed from the workforce.

COMMUNIST POLICIES ON FAMILY, 1917-1941

Communist policies on the family saw experimentation in the 1920s and a return to traditional values in the 1930s.

What was the communist view on family?

The communist view of family changed over time. Initially, they saw the traditional family as unnecessary and bourgeois. However, Stalin's *(p.121)* Great Retreat *(p.111)* in 1936 saw the return of more traditional views about family.

What policies on family did the communists introduce?

The communists brought in 4 main policies which affected the family:

- ☑ In 1918, the Family Code said the state would provide child care and social services as the family was no longer necessary. Divorce was made easier, abortion was legalised and créches were made available.
- ☑ In 1927, new marriage laws meant that unregistered marriages and registered marriages had equal status.
- ☑ In 1936, Stalin *(p.121)* returned to traditional family values in his Great Retreat *(p.111)* which made divorce more expensive, and both male homosexuality and abortion were made illegal.
- ☑ In July 1944, the status of family was increased again, as a tax on single people was introduced and women who had ten or more children received the 'Mother Heroine' award.

What were the results of the communists' policies on family?

The communists' policies on family had mixed results:

- ☑ The initial policy of 1918 had unintended consequences because it encouraged divorce and family breakdown resulting in an increase in single mothers and abandoned children. By the mid-1920s the USSR had the highest divorce rate in Europe.
- ☑ It led to social problems with gangs of orphans roaming the streets.
- ☑ Stalin's *(p.121)* Great Retreat *(p.111)* led to a 28% increase in births from 1931 to 1940.

COMMUNIST POLICIES ON ART AND CULTURE, 1917-1941

Art and culture were to reinforce socialist views and help create new Soviet men and women.

What was the communist view on art and culture?

The Communist Party felt art and culture should create the 'new Soviet man' - an ideal socialist who thought and acted according to socialist values. This would completely remove and destroy the culture of tsarist Russia.

How was art and culture controlled under Bolshevik rule?

Under the communist government there was control in 3 main ways through censorship and propaganda:

- ☑ The Commissariat of Enlightenment was set up in 1917, under the leadership of Anatoly Lunacharsky, to support and encourage artists to work with the communist government. Initially, under Lenin, it allowed experimentation; under Stalin *(p.121)*, it was used to control artists.
- ☑ Banned books were removed from libraries and schools.
- ☑ All publications, including newspapers and magazines, had to be approved by the government censorship office.

What was the Proletkult movement in communist art and culture?

The Proletkult was:

- ☑ A movement supported by Anatoly Lunacharsky, the head of the Commissariat of Enlightenment, and Alexander Bogdanov.
- ☑ An attempt to create the USSR's own proletarian culture to promote communist values.
- ☑ It began in 1918 and was replaced by social realism under Stalin *(p.121)* from the 1930s.

What was the avant-garde movement in communist art and culture?

The avant-garde movement in art and culture:

- ☑ Challenged traditional art and encouraged experimentation.
- ☑ It included Modernism and Futurism - art that conveyed images of the future.
- ☑ It was a popular art movement after the First World War and saw avant-garde films created such as 'Battleship Potemkin' in 1925 by the director, Eisenstein.

What was socialist realism in communist art and culture?

Socialist realism *(p.93)*:

- ☑ Was a type of art which portrayed life under socialism in a positive way.
- ☑ Tended to portray ordinary people in ordinary situations, such as work, mines and schools, as heroes.
- ☑ Became the only acceptable form of art under Stalin's *(p.121)* rule from the 1930s onwards.

DID YOU KNOW?

The 1920s was a period of experimentation in Russian arts and culture.

Some experimentation did not work. One play, Mystery Bouffe, was cancelled after 3 performances as the audience struggled to understand it.

COMMUNIST POLICIES ON RELIGION, 1917-1941

Communists are atheists.

 What was the communist view on religion?

Communists are atheists; they do not believe in religion. They saw it as a threat to communism because the Russian Orthodox Church had power, position and status.

 What was Lenin's view of religion in communist Russia?

Lenin was very anti-religion and pursued policies to remove the influence of the Church in the USSR.

 What was Stalin's view on religion in communist Russia?

Stalin *(p.121)* was anti-religion and wanted to remove the influence of the Church in the USSR. However, he was more pragmatic than Lenin. During the Second World War he allowed the Church to have more influence to help the country.

 How did the communists control religion?

The Communist Party brought in 4 main measures to control the Church and religion:

☑ In January 1918, the Decree Concerning Separation of Church and State was issued. This closed church schools, stopped state subsidies and nationalised church property.

☑ In 1918, the Decree on Freedom of Conscience separated the Church from state. The Church lost land, religious publications were banned, and religious education outside home was banned.

☑ There were attacks on priests and churches under Lenin and Stalin *(p.121)*. In Stalin's Great Purge, there were quotas for how many priests should be purged.

☑ During the Second World War, Stalin *(p.121)* relaxed the persecution of religion for pragmatic reasons to support people. Churches reopened to give comfort to families.

What was the communist attitude towards the Jewish religion?

Stalin's *(p.121)* treatment of Jews worsened over time in 6 main ways:

☑ All decrees which controlled religion affected Jewish people as well.

☑ After the Second World War, Stalin's *(p.121)* anti-Semitism grew and attacks increased.

☑ Jewish people were sacked from government posts and industry if they held any responsibility.

☑ There was a purge of Jewish leaders and some were executed.

☑ The government made it very difficult for Jewish people to emigrate to Israel.

☑ Many Jewish institutions such as schools were closed.

DID YOU KNOW?

Many beautiful Russian Orthodox churches were destroyed or used for other purposes.

One example is the beautiful cathedral of Christ the Saviour in Moscow, which was demolished to make way for a new 'Palace of the Soviets'. The new building was cancelled due to the Second World War braking out and the site was instead used for a swimming pool - at the time, the largest in the world!

Quizzes, amazing exam preparation tools and more at GCSEHistory.com

HOW STALIN WON THE LEADERSHIP STRUGGLE, 1924-1929

Stalin slowly outmanoeuvred his political opponents in the leadership struggle.

What was the leadership struggle in Russia?

After the death of Lenin in 1924, Stalin *(p.121)* ultimately won the leadership contest to rule Russia. He used different methods to do this, including using the power he had from his position as general secretary, playing his rivals off against each other, and using a pragmatic approach to win.

When did Stalin defeat his rivals in the leadership struggle in Russia?

Stalin *(p.121)* defeated his rivals in the leadership struggle between 1924 and 1929.

Who were Stalin's rivals in leadership struggle in Russia?

Stalin's *(p.121)* rivals in the leadership struggle after Lenin's death were: Trotsky, Kamenev, Zinoviev and Bukharin.

Why was there a leadership struggle in Russia after Lenin's death?

There was no clear successor to Lenin after he died. Lenin had not left instructions as to who should be the new leader of the Communist Party, nor who would lead the USSR. Therefore, there was a power struggle between 5 different candidates.

What did Lenin say about the individuals involved in the Russian leadership struggle?

Lenin wrote his 'Testament' in December 1922, after his second stroke, as he realised he was likely to die soon. In it, he criticised all of the men who might replace him. Lenin said:

- ☑ Trotsky was the most capable, but far too arrogant.
- ☑ Stalin *(p.121)* was too powerful, too rude, and he should be dismissed as party secretary.
- ☑ Kamenev had not supported Lenin's October Revolution *(p.56)*, and so should not be trusted.
- ☑ Zinoviev had not supported Lenin's October Revolution *(p.56)*, and so should not be trusted.
- ☑ Bukharin was the favourite of the party members, but Lenin felt he did not fully understand Marxism.

What did Stalin do first in the leadership struggle in the Soviet Union?

Stalin *(p.121)* immediately acted strategically in 4 main ways to secure the leadership of the Soviet Union:

- ☑ He organised Lenin's funeral and carried his coffin to present himself as a close friend and loyal supporter.
- ☑ Trotsky did not attend the funeral. He claimed Stalin *(p.121)* deliberately told him the incorrect date so it would appear as if he didn't respect Lenin.
- ☑ In May 1924, Kamenev, Zinoviev and Stalin *(p.121)* all agreed to not release Lenin's 'Testament', the document dictated by Lenin in December 1922.
- ☑ This meant fewer people knew about Lenin's criticisms of the members of the Communist Party who were candidates to become the new leader. This included the harsh criticisms of Stalin *(p.121)*.

What was the split in the Communist Party that Stalin exploited in the leadership struggle in Russia?

The Communist Party was split between the left wing and the right wing:

- ☑ The right wing wanted to continue the New Economic Policy to slowly industrialise and favoured the idea of socialism in one country, ie building communism in the USSR.
- ☑ The left wing wanted to abandon the NEP, and have rapid industrialisation and worldwide revolution.

How did Stalin eliminate his rivals in the leadership struggle in Russia?

Stalin *(p.121)* was very clever. He divided and conquered his rivals in 3 stages:

- Stage 1: Stalin *(p.121)* united with Zinoviev and Kamenev to attack and isolate Trotsky.
- Stage 2: Stalin *(p.121)* united with Bukharin to attack the United Opposition of Zinoviev, Kamenev and Trotsky.
- Stage 3: Stalin *(p.121)* turned on Bukharin to attack the Right Opposition.

How did Stalin eliminate his rivals in the leadership struggle in Stage 1 in Russia?

Stalin *(p.121)* took 3 key actions in Stage 1:

- In 1924, Stalin *(p.121)* allied with Zinoviev and Kamenev to remove Trotsky. They supported the New Economic Policy against Trotsky, who supported rapid industrialisation.
- Zinoviev and Kamenev undermined Trotsky and worked against him at the Thirteenth Party Congress in 1924 so that all of his ideas were rejected.
- As a result, Trotsky lost his job as Commissar for War in 1925.

How did Stalin eliminate his rivals in the leadership struggle in Stage 2 in Russia?

Stalin *(p.121)* took 4 key actions in Stage 2:

- In 1927, Stalin *(p.121)* allied with Bukharin and supported the NEP against the United Opposition of Zinoviev, Kamenev and Trotsky.
- The United Opposition hoped to gain support for their ideas of rapid industrialisation and world revolution at the Fifteenth Party Congress in 1927.
- Stalin *(p.121)* accused Trotsky, Zinoviev and Kamenev of 'factionalism' which Lenin had banned in 1921. This was because they had formed a group which was against the party's New Economic Policy.
- Therefore, Trotsky, Zinoviev and Kamenev were expelled from the party in 1927. Trotsky withdrew from Soviet politics and went into exile.

How did Stalin eliminate his rivals in the leadership struggle in Stage 3 in Russia?

Stalin *(p.121)* took 3 key actions in Stage 3:

- In 1928, he switched his support to rapid industrialisation, attacking Bukharin and the Right Opposition.
- Bukharin disagreed with Stalin *(p.121)* over abandoning the New Economic Policy, and began plotting with Kamenev to stop him.
- Bukharin's plotting was discovered and he was expelled from the Politburo *(p.71)* in 1929.

Why was Stalin able to win the leadership struggle in 1929 in Russia?

There were 7 important reasons why Stalin *(p.121)* won the power struggle in 1929:

- His rivals made mistakes.
- Stalin *(p.121)* was able to exploit the division in the party over policy choices. Stalin switched his allegiance from the NEP to rapid industrialisation to attack his rivals.
- Being the general secretary meant Stalin *(p.121)* could put his supporters into positions that mattered, such as the Party Congress, to vote against his rivals.
- Stalin *(p.121)* was a very clever politician. He used his position as general secretary to undermine his rivals and he switched alliances to benefit his own position.
- He used his position as general secretary to pack the Thirteenth Party Congress in 1924 and the Fifteenth Party Congress in 1927 with his supporters.
- He took a pragmatic approach to policy. He supported Lenin's New Economic Policy between 1924 and 1928, when it appeared to be working, so he could attack the Left Opposition, but he switched to supporting rapid industrialisation in 1928 when NEP was becoming unpopular.
- He was lucky. For example, in 1923 when Lenin was dying, Trotsky also fell ill and was unable to compete with Stalin *(p.121)*.

What mistakes did Stalin's rivals make in the leadership struggle in Russia?

Stalin's *(p.121)* rivals made 2 key mistakes:

☑ Zinoviev and Kamenev had trusted Stalin *(p.121)* and worked with him to keep Trotsky out of power.

☑ Zinoviev and Kamenev agreed to not publish Lenin's 'Testament', which had severely criticised Stalin *(p.121)*.

What mistakes did Trotsky make during the leadership struggle in Russia?

Trotsky made six key mistakes which helped Stalin *(p.121)* to defeat him:

☑ Trotsky did not attend Lenin's funeral, did not insist that Lenin's 'Testament' was published and was not popular with the Party members.

☑ Many members of the party were offended by Trotsky's arrogant attitude. Some were concerned because he had such an influential role in the Red Army.

☑ He failed to take the opposition seriously.

☑ He underestimated Stalin *(p.121)* as a politician and was more concerned with the other contenders.

☑ Other party members did not agree with Trotsky's idea of permanent revolution because it could potentially drag the USSR into future conflict.

☑ There were concerns that his radical policies might split the party.

What was the title of the leader of the USSR after the leadership struggle in Russia?

When Stalin *(p.121)* had eliminated his rivals and took control of the country, he kept his existing title, General Secretary of the Communist Party of the Soviet Union.

DID YOU KNOW?

Stalin was born Josef Vissarionovich Djugashvili.

He changed his name to Stalin, from the Russian for 'man of steel'.

CONTENDERS IN THE LEADERSHIP STRUGGLE, 1924-1929

There was no clear successor when Lenin died.

 ## What were the strengths of the contenders in the leadership struggle in Russia?

The contenders in the struggle for the leadership of Russia all had their own unique strengths and weaknesses. Any of them could have succeeded Lenin.

 ## What were the strengths of Stalin as a contender in the leadership struggle in Russia?

Stalin *(p.121)* had 6 main strengths:

☑ He was the general secretary of the party in 1922, which gave him a lot of power as he could control what was discussed in the Politburo *(p.71)* meetings.

☑ He could appoint his supporters to key jobs because he was general secretary.

☑ He had access to 26,000 personal files which he could use against the other contenders.

☑ He launched the Lenin Enrolment programme from 1923 to 1925. This recruited over 500,000 largely uneducated and poor members who were loyal to him.

☑ Many members favoured his idea of socialism in one country, where they would concentrate on developing communism in the USSR rather than worldwide.

☑ Most of the leading communists underestimated Stalin *(p.121)* and viewed him as merely a capable administrator.

 What were the weaknesses of Stalin as a contender in the leadership struggle in Russia?

Stalin *(p.121)* had 4 main weaknesses:

☑ Stalin *(p.121)* was harshly criticised by Lenin in his 'Testament'. If this became public knowledge it would undermine him.

☑ He had angered Lenin by being very rude to Lenin's wife, Krupskaya.

☑ He did not take part in the October Revolution *(p.56)*.

☑ He was not popular or well-known in the party, considering his relatively high level of responsibility within it. He had been famously described as 'the grey blur' - a bureaucrat and administrator, rather than a charismatic leader.

 What were Trotsky's strengths as a contender in the leadership struggle in Russia?

Trotsky had 4 main strengths:

☑ He played a significant role in the October Revolution *(p.56)*, working closely with Lenin.

☑ He enabled the communists to win the civil war by creating the Red Army.

☑ He was a great speaker and organiser.

☑ He was popular with the younger and more radical members.

 What were Trotsky's weaknesses as a contender in the leadership struggle in Russia?

Trotsky had 3 key weaknesses:

☑ He joined the Communist Party in 1917, so he was not seen as one of the 'Old Bolsheviks *(p.32)*'.

☑ He was disliked by members of the party because he was Jewish and seen as arrogant and rude.

☑ Many members did not like his idea of worldwide revolution because it meant a continued struggle and possible war

 What were Kamenev's strengths as a contender in the leadership struggle in Russia?

Kamenev 2 main strengths were:

☑ He had joined the party in 1903, so he was seen as an 'Old Bolshevik *(p.32)*'.

☑ He was the party secretary in Moscow, which gave him a power base.

 What were Kamenev's weaknesses as a contender in the leadership struggle in Russia?

Kamenev's 2 key weaknesses were:

☑ He was seen as disloyal to Lenin because he had opposed Lenin's plans for the timing of the October Revolution *(p.56)*

☑ He was not really involved in the civil war.

 What were Zinoviev's strengths as a leadership contender in Russia?

Zinoviev's 3 main strengths were:

☑ He had a strong party base because he was the party secretary in Leningrad.

☑ He was considered an 'Old Bolshevik *(p.32)*' because he joined the party in 1903.

☑ He was a close friend of Lenin.

 What were Zinoviev's weaknesses as a contender in the leadership contender in Russia?

Zinoviev's 3 key weaknesses were:

☑ He was seen as disloyal to Lenin because he had opposed Lenin's plans for the timing of the October Revolution *(p.56)*

- ☑ He was not heavily involved in the civil war.
- ☑ He was seen as ineffectual.

 What were Bukharin's strengths as a contender for leadership in Russia?

Bukharin's 4 main strengths were:

- ☑ Lenin described him as the 'golden boy' of the Communist Party - he was very popular.
- ☑ He supported Lenin until his death.
- ☑ He played an important role in the Communist Party between 1925 and 1928.
- ☑ He was the editor of the communist newspaper, Pravda.

 What were Bukharin's weaknesses as a contender in the leadership struggle in Russia?

Bukharin's 3 main weaknesses were:

- ☑ He had disagreed with Lenin over the ending of the First World War and the signing of the Treaty of Brest-Litovsk *(p.63)*.
- ☑ He supported the New Economic Policy, which made him unpopular with the party's left wing.
- ☑ He was seen as too young and inexperienced.

DID YOU KNOW?

Stalin went on to remove Trotsky from photos where he was shown with Lenin to give the impression the two had never been close.

THE PURGES, OR GREAT TERROR, 1930S

Stalin's paranoia reached new heights in the Great Purge.

 What were the purges?

The Soviet purges involved the mass arrests, imprisonment and executions of political prisoners, dissidents and people considered a threat to Stalin *(p.121)*.

 When were the purges?

The Great Purge, also known as the Great Terror, took place between 1936 and 1938.

 Who was in charge of carrying out the purges?

The purges were carried out by the secret police, or the People's Commissariat of Internal Affairs (NKVD *(p.89)*) under the leadership of:

- ☑ Yagoda from 1934 to 1936.
- ☑ Yezhov from 1936 to 1938.

 Who was targeted by the purges?

A wide range of groups were targeted as 'enemies of the people':

- ☑ Members of the Communist Party, in particular Old Bolsheviks *(p.32)* who had worked with Lenin, such as Kamenev and Zinoviev.

- ☑ Leading members in the Central Committee.
- ☑ The armed forces.
- ☑ Artists, writers and musicians.
- ☑ Kulaks.
- ☑ Priests.
- ☑ Scientists.

 What were the reasons for the purges?

There were political and economic reasons for the purges.

 What were the political reasons for the purges?

There were 8 political reasons for the purges:

- ☑ Stalin *(p. 121)* was paranoid and he saw enemies and opposition everywhere.
- ☑ It would give Stalin *(p. 121)* total control of the Communist Party and the country.
- ☑ People were incredibly unhappy because of the negative impact of collectivisation and industrialisation so there was more political opposition.
- ☑ There was growing political opposition in the Communist Party because of Stalin's *(p. 121)* policies of rapid industrialisation and collectivisation.
- ☑ One leading Party member, Ryutin, openly criticised Stalin *(p. 121)* in 1932. However, when Stalin demanded the death penalty, the Politburo *(p. 71)*, including Kirov, voted against it.
- ☑ At the 17th Party Congress in 1934, Kirov, a member of the Politburo *(p. 71)*, spoke out against rapid collectivisation and received a longer standing ovation than Stalin *(p. 121)*.
- ☑ Kirov received more votes than Stalin *(p. 121)* in the elections to the Central Committee so he had become a threat to Stalin's position as general secretary of the Party.
- ☑ On 1st December 1934, Sergei Kirov, was murdered and Stalin *(p. 121)* claimed Kamenev, Zinoviev and Trotsky were to blame and used it as an excuse to start the purges.

 What were the economic reasons for the purges?

There were 3 main economic reasons for the purges:

- ☑ Those targeted could be blamed for the economic issues, for example missed targets.
- ☑ Economically, the purges helped Stalin *(p. 121)* as they provided free labour from the gulags.
- ☑ The fear created by the purges could be used as a weapon to pressure people into meeting their economic targets.

 What were the show trials during the purges?

Show trials were an important part of the purge:

- ☑ They were held for those with a high profile and people Stalin *(p. 121)* viewed as an enemy.
- ☑ The scripts were written beforehand and everyone already knew what the outcome would be.
- ☑ The accused were tortured into confessing, often to save their families.

 When were the show trials during the purges?

The show trials occurred between 1936 and 1938.

 Which were the most important show trials during the purges?

There three trials that were the most important:

- ☑ Trial of 16 in August 1936, which included Zinoviev and Kamenev.
- ☑ Trial of 17 in January 1937, of party officials.

☑ Trial of 21 in March 1938, which included Bukharin and Yagoda (ex-head of the NKVD *(p.89)*).

 What happened during the Trial of 16 during the purges?

The following 3 key events happened during the Trial of 16, in 1936:

☑ 16 people, including Zinoviev and Kamenev, were accused of disrupting the Five Year Plans and Kirov's murder.

☑ They were tortured and threatened so they would confess.

☑ They were executed.

 What happened during the Trial of 17 during the purges?

The following 3 key events happened during the Trial of 17, in 1937:

☑ Party officials were accused of plotting to overthrow the government, disrupting the Five Year Plans and Kirov's murder.

☑ They were tortured and threatened so they would confess.

☑ Thirteen were executed and 4 sent to the Gulags.

 What happened during the Trial of 21 during the purges?

The following 4 key events happened during the Trial of 21, in 1938:

☑ 21 people, including Bukharin and Yagoda (ex-head of the NKVD *(p.89)*), were accused of plotting to overthrow the government, disrupting the Five Year Plans and Kirov's murder.

☑ They were tortured and threatened so they would confess.

☑ Bukharin attempted to speak out against show trials to prove that the trials were false and unjust.

☑ Again, the accused were executed.

 What happened during the Great Purge?

There were 7 key events during the Great Purge:

☑ There were mass arrests, forced confessions and people were either executed or imprisoned in a Gulag *(p.90)*.

☑ The show trials of 1936 to 1938.

☑ The NKVD *(p.89)* relied on ordinary people to inform on their neighbours.

☑ Between 1936 and 1938, the terror escalated under the NKVD *(p.89)* leader, Yezhov. This period is called Yezhovshchina.

☑ From May 1937, the armed forces were purged starting with 8 generals, including Marshal Tukhachevsky, who was accused of plotting against Stalin *(p.121)*.

☑ In July 1937, Yezhov passed NKVD *(p.89)* Order 00447. This set quotas for how many people had to be arrested, of whom 28% were shot and the rest sent to Gulags.

☑ By the end of the purge of the military, all naval admirals and all but one air force commander had been executed, along with the majority of the army's command.

 Why were many of the Old Bolsheviks executed during the purges?

Many 'Old Bolsheviks *(p.32)*' who were part of the October 1917 revolution were killed during the purges because it enabled Stalin *(p.121)* to consolidate his position as the dictator of both the Communist Party and the USSR. Bukharin and Kamenev were among those he executed.

 Why did the purges end?

There were 2 main reasons why Stalin *(p.121)* halted the purges by the end of 1938:

☑ They had destabilised society and were escalating out of control as neighbour turned on neighbour.

☑ They were disrupting the economy to such an extent that the targets of the Five Year Plans were not being met because key workers were caught up in the terror.

 ## What were the results of the Great Purge?

The impact of the purges was significant in 4 main ways:

☑ The cost in human life was horrific, with an estimated 7 to 8 million arrested, 2 million dead in the gulags, and 1 to 1.5 million executed.

☑ Politically, Stalin *(p.121)* had created a personal dictatorship in which any opposition from within the party or outside had been killed off.

☑ Economically, the purges were a huge disruption as the experienced people needed to meet the targets of the Five Year Plans were removed from their jobs.

☑ Militarily, the purges meant that the USSR was less able to fight Nazi Germany when they invaded in 1941.

 ## Were there purges during the Second World War?

There were 2 key purges during the Second World War:

☑ The Volga Germans were considered suspect when the Nazis invaded the USSR in 1941. Therefore, they were deported to Siberia.

☑ The USSR deported ethnic Finns and internally placed them in exile when Finland supported the Nazi invasion of the USSR.

 ## Who was targeted in purges after the Second World War?

There were 4 key groups that were purged after the Second World War:

☑ Nationalists.

☑ Soldiers who were German prisoners of war.

☑ The Leningrad Communist Party.

☑ Jews.

 ## How were the Jews purged after the Second World War?

The Jews were purged after the Second World War in 3 key ways:

☑ Any Jewish person in a position of responsibility lost their job.

☑ Leaders of the Jewish community were arrested.

☑ In 1953, Stalin *(p.121)* claimed there was a 'Doctor's Plot' in which 10 Jewish doctors were plotting to assassinate him. It led to mass arrests but Stalin died before anything else happened.

 ## What were the purges of soldiers after the Second World War?

After the Second World War, Soviet soldiers that had been German Prisoners of War were purged:

☑ 1.5 million Soviet soldiers that had been held as prisoners of war by Nazi Germany were returned to the USSR.

☑ They were considered traitors and deported to the Gulags in Siberia.

 ## What were the purges of nationalists after the Second World War?

After the Second World War, nationalists were purged in 3 main ways:

☑ Some of the USSR's republics attempted to win their independence at the end of the war.

☑ Lithuania, Ukraine, Estonia and Latvia had all taken up arms against the USSR.

☑ In response, there were mass deportations.

How was the Communist Party purged after the Second World War?

After the Second World War, the Communist Party was purged:

- ☑ In 1949, Stalin *(p.121)* attacked the top party officials of the Leningrad Communist Party because he thought it was a threat.
- ☑ 200 members were arrested on charges of spying for Britain and corruption. Some members were shot, some were imprisoned and some were exiled.
- ☑ About 2,000 officials also lost their jobs.

DID YOU KNOW?

Nikolai Yezhov was the leader of the NKVD when Great Purge escalated between 1936 and 1938.

He was nicknamed the 'Poisoned Dwarf' and some say he attended meetings with blood on his shirt after torturing his victims.

THE SECRET POLICE, INCLUDING THE NKVD

The secret police had unimaginable power in the USSR.

 Who were the secret police in the USSR?

The secret police was an organisation which had the job of eliminating any opposition to communist rule.

 What were the secret police known as in the USSR?

The secret police were variously known as:

- ☑ The Cheka, or All-Russian Extraordinary Committee to Combat Counter-Revolution and Sabotage, from 1917 to 1922.
- ☑ The GPU, or State Political Directorate, in 1922.
- ☑ The OGPU, or All-Union State Political Board, from 1923.
- ☑ The NKVD, or People's Commissariat for Internal Affairs, from 1934 to 1953.
- ☑ KGB or ,Committee for State Security, from 1954.

 What was the Soviet secret police's primary responsibility?

The secret police removed and suppressed all opposition:

- ☑ The Cheka committed the Red Terror *(p.68)* during the Civil War.
- ☑ They participated in the attack on the kulaks during collectivisation.
- ☑ The NKVD carried out the Great Purge under Stalin *(p.121)*.

 What were the techniques of the Soviet Secret Police?

The secret police in the USSR used 4 main - and extreme - techniques:

- ☑ Mass arrests.
- ☑ Forced confessions under torture.
- ☑ Development of informant networks.

☑ Quotas were introduced in July 1937, with Order 00447 setting out how many arrests the NKVD was expected to make and how many people should be executed.

> ### DID YOU KNOW?
>
> **The secret police operated outside the legal system in the USSR until after Stalin's death.**
>
> This meant it could act in ways considered illegal without being held accountable.

THE GULAGS

The gulags were a key tool of political repression and provided slave labour for the economy.

What were the gulags?

The Gulag was the government organisation established by Lenin to run forced labour camps. The camps themselves were also called gulags, after the name of the agency that set them up.

When were the gulags started?

The Gulag system was set up under Lenin in 1919.

What was the gulags' purpose?

There were 3 key reasons why the gulags were created:

☑ As a form of severe punishment.

☑ A way in which to get free labour from the inmates.

☑ As a deterrent to other people.

How did the Gulag system grow?

The Gulag system grew over time in 4 main stages:

☑ In 1919, the first gulags were opened under Lenin.

☑ In 1921, there were 84 camps.

☑ In 1929, there were approximately 179,000 prisoners.

☑ By 1950, there were approximately 2.5 million prisoners.

Who was put in the gulags?

The gulags were set up to accommodate 7 main groups of prisoners accused of a wide range of crimes:

☑ Political prisoners, such as those accused of plotting to overthrow the government and foreign communists accused of spying.

☑ Peasants, especially Kulaks, accused of sabotaging collectivisation.

☑ Workers and factory managers convicted of disrupting factory work and production.

☑ Leaders of different ethnic groups who wanted independence from the USSR.

☑ Ordinary criminals.

☑ Members of the armed forces.

☑ Any artists, writers or educators who were considered a threat.

Where were the gulags?

The gulags were particularly prevalent in the east of the Soviet Union, especially in Siberia.

How did the Soviet Union profit from the gulags?

The gulags provided a huge amount of slave labour, with prisoners forced to work in industry, on the massive industrial projects such as Moscow's metro and the White Sea Canal, and on the railways.

What were the conditions of the gulags?

Conditions in the gulags were terrible in 5 main ways:

- ☑ Food was rationed and tied to how much work prisoners completed.
- ☑ Rations were cut if prisoners did not meet their targets and so many prisoners died of starvation. Extra rations could be earned by working harder.
- ☑ The work was hard labour and tied to the targets of the Five Year Plans.
- ☑ Many prisoners died due to the work as it was so dangerous and difficult.
- ☑ The living conditions were awful; over crowded, with little sanitation and no heating. Many died of the cold.

DID YOU KNOW?

Gulag is an acronym for Glavnoe Upravlenie Lagerei.
This is Russian for 'Main Camp Administration'.

SOVIET PROPAGANDA UNDER STALIN

Soviet propaganda was a key feature of Stalin's government.

What was Soviet Union propaganda under Stalin?

Propaganda is information which tends to be deliberately biased or misleading, and it is used to promote a certain point of view. The Soviet government used propaganda to make its people believe certain things or have certain attitudes.

Why did the Soviet Union use propaganda?

Soviet propaganda had 2 key aims:

- ☑ To control the people of the Soviet Union.
- ☑ The Soviet government wanted to create the 'new Soviet man' and the 'new Soviet women' who would show desirable Socialist qualities e.g. care more about the community than the individual.

What methods of propaganda did the Soviet Union use?

There were 7 main methods of propaganda:

- ☑ Stalin's *(p.121)* cult of personality *(p.95)* used all forms of the media to create a specific image of Stalin as a heroic and all-knowing leader.
- ☑ All art and culture was controlled and the only official culture allowed was socialist realism *(p.93)*.
- ☑ Through different organisations such as the youth group, the Komsomol, or through education.
- ☑ By rewriting history and changing facts to suit the Soviet cause.

- ☑ All books, newspapers and magazines were controlled and written to support the Soviet government.
- ☑ Photographs were altered to suit the Soviet government's view of events.
- ☑ Radios were put up in public places such as work and clubs in the 1920s for group listening.

DID YOU KNOW?

The Communist Party used propaganda from the time of the revolutions through to the collapse of the USSR in 1991.

During the Civil War, Trotsky organised the Agitprop trains to spread the communist message across the country.

SOVIET CENSORSHIP UNDER STALIN

Soviet censorship was extensive; all information had to be controlled.

What was censorship under Stalin?

Censorship is the control of information in the media which could be considered unacceptable by the government. Under Stalin's *(p. 121)* rule, the Soviet government had very strict control of information in terms of what people could see, hear or read.

Why did Stalin use censorship?

There were 3 main reasons why Stalin *(p. 121)* used censorship:

- ☑ To control what people knew.
- ☑ To stop any criticism of him or the government.
- ☑ To stop any opposition developing or having the ability to undermine the government.

How did the communists implement censorship of the media?

There were 6 important ways to censor information:

- ☑ Lenin had banned all non-Bolshevik newspapers in 1917.
- ☑ The radio was also controlled by the Commission for Posts and Telegraph.
- ☑ Printing presses were nationalised by Lenin.
- ☑ The Communist Party had its own newspaper, Pravda (Truth).
- ☑ The Soviet government had its own newspaper called the Izvestiya (News).
- ☑ The government controlled what could be published using the Censorship Office or Glavlit which was controlled by the secret police.

How did censorship affect Soviet art and culture?

Censorship had a negative impact on art and culture as the quality of what was produced was reduced. Some artists refused to create any work.

What happened to people who broke the censorship laws in the Soviet Union?

Writers, journalists, artists or anyone who broke the censorship laws were punished in 2 main ways:

- ☑ They could be internally exiled which meant being sent to live in a different part of the USSR.
- ☑ They could be sent to a gulag. *(p.90)*

SOCIALIST REALISM

Stalin favoured Socialist Realism in art and literature.

❓ What was the communist policy of socialist realism?

Socialist realism was a communist policy on art and culture which portrayed life under socialism in a positive way. It was focused on ordinary people.

⌛ When was the communist policy of socialist realism in force?

Socialist realism was official Communist Party policy from the 1930 to 1953 under Stalin's *(p.121)* rule.

👤 Who was involved with the communist policy of socialist realism?

There were different people involved with the socialist realism movement:

- ☑ Stalin *(p.121)* ordered that all art and culture should follow the artistic style of socialist realism.
- ☑ The film director, Eisenstein, was very popular.
- ☑ In literature, writers Sholokhov, (1928's 'And Quiet Flows the Don'), and Kataev, (1932's 'Time Forward'), were popular.

🏅 How did the communist policy of socialist realism affect art?

Under socialist realism, art:

- ☑ Often showed peasants with plentiful harvests and successful industrial workers.
- ☑ Became part of Stalin's *(p.121)* cult of personality *(p.95)*.
- ☑ Showed happy and positive images of ordinary life in the Soviet Union.

🏅 How did the communist policy of socialist realism affect music and dance?

Under socialist realism, music and dance:

- ☑ Traditional folk music and dancing as well as ballet dancing were encouraged.
- ☑ Jazz music was banned.

🏅 How did the communist policy of socialist realism affect literature?

Under socialist realism, literature was:

- ☑ Focused on ordinary workers or peasants.
- ☑ Centred on life in the Soviet Union, such as a record-breaking shift in the steel factories or life on a collective farm. War and detective stories were also popular.

How did the communist policy of socialist realism affect cinema?

Under socialist realism, the cinema focused on glorious tales from Soviet or Russian history, such as the Russian Civil War *(p.65)*.

1936 CONSTITUTION

In reality, the 1936 Soviet Constitution did not give citizens any rights.

What was the Stalin Constitution?

The 1936 Soviet Constitution, also known as the Stalin *(p.121)* Constitution, redesigned the government of the Soviet Union.

When was the Stalin Constitution adopted?

The 1936 Soviet Constitution was adopted on 5th December, 1936.

Why was the constitution changed by Stalin?

The new constitution was introduced for 2 main reasons:

- ✅ To show the Soviet Union had changed since the 1924 constitution.
- ✅ In an attempt to improve the USSR's reputation with other countries.

What did the 1936 constitution include?

The 1936 Soviet Constitution include the following 5 main articles:

- ✅ It granted different rights and freedoms, such as the right to vote from the age of 18, to housing, and to care in old age and illness.
- ✅ It established direct elections of the government.
- ✅ It changed the name of the Central Executive Committee to the Supreme Soviet.
- ✅ Groups previously seen as enemies, such as the nobility and kulaks, would be seen as equal citizens.
- ✅ All of the 15 republics were renamed as Soviet Socialist Republics under Article 13. They were given the impression of a degree of autonomy but in reality they were controlled from Moscow.

What impact did the 1936 constitution have?

The 1936 Constitution had little impact due to 3 main reasons:

- ✅ It was a piece of propaganda.
- ✅ The rights were not upheld as there were still mass arrests and the government used terror to control the population.
- ✅ Only Communist Party members could be elected to government.

STALIN'S CULT OF PERSONALITY

Stalin's cult of personality encouraged people to worship him almost as though he were a god.

What was Stalin's cult of personality?

Stalin *(p.121)* wanted to be praised and adored. A 'cult of personality' was developed for him in the USSR to create adoration of him through the use or art and popular culture to improve his status as the leader and to inspire loyalty.

When did Stalin's cult of personality exist?

Stalin's *(p.121)* cult of personality developed in the 1920s and existed throughout his time as leader of the USSR.

Why was there a cult of Stalin?

There were 4 important reasons why Stalin *(p.121)* developed his cult of personality:

- ✅ To increase Stalin's *(p.121)* legitimacy and authority as Lenin's true successor.
- ✅ To unify the USSR around loyalty to one leader. This was a tradition in tsarist Russia where the tsar *(p.19)* was seen as 'the little father'. Stalin's *(p.121)* cult of personality was an extension of this.
- ✅ It raised Stalin's *(p.121)* status above other members of the Party so he became all powerful.
- ✅ Rapid industrialisation and collectivisation had created great suffering in the USSR. The cult of personality could be used to direct dissatisfaction towards other leaders in the Communist Party, not Stalin *(p.121)*.

What was Stalin's image according to his cult of personality?

Stalin *(p.121)* had 4 main characteristics according to his cult.

- ✅ Stalin *(p.121)* was portrayed as a man of the people working alongside ordinary people. He was characterised as a 'father-figure', very much in the style of the tsars.
- ✅ He was portrayed as an economic expert and amazing economic planner. All forms of media sung the praises of Stalin *(p.121)* and his Five Year Plans.
- ✅ He was presented as a great thinker who understood communism and who was the true successor of Lenin. He was called 'Vozhd' which means leader.
- ✅ Stalin's *(p.121)* cult of personality developed after the Second World War. He became the 'Generalissimo' which portrayed him as the saviour of the USSR. Films depicted him as a hero; for example, he was shown defeating the Nazis in Berlin when he was never actually there.

How was Stalin's cult of personality created?

There were 4 key ways in which Stalin's *(p.121)* cult of personality was created:

- ✅ All images showed Stalin *(p.121)* in a positive way. Posters, paintings, photographs and films created a myth of Stalin as a hero.

- ✅ Stalin *(p.121)* was honoured in numerous ways. Towns, streets and buildings were named after him. There were statues of him in most towns and cities.
- ✅ History was rewritten to emphasise Stalin's *(p.121)* contribution to key events such as the October Revolution *(p.56)* in 1917. Old photographs were altered to rewrite history.
- ✅ Stalin *(p.121)* was given many titles such as 'Brilliant Genius of Humanity'.

DID YOU KNOW?

The impact of cult was so far-reaching that when Stalin died in 1953 there was outpouring of grief, despite the fact he ruled over a country in which millions were murdered in the Great Terror.

HOW FAR HAD STALIN CONSOLIDATED HIS POSITION BY 1941?

'He established unity in the Soviet Union. He consolidated what Lenin had begun: party unity. He gave the international revolutionary movement a new impetus. The USSR's industrialization was one of Stalin's wisest actions.' - Fidel Castro in 1992, describing Stalin's rule

❓ What did Stalin do to consolidate his power?

Stalin *(p.121)* had consolidated his hold on power by 1941 and created a personal dictatorship in the USSR. However, he did not have have complete control over the USSR.

How did Stalin consolidate his power by 1941?

Stalin *(p.121)* used 4 main methods to consolidate his power by 1941:

- ✅ The purges of the 1930s.
- ✅ His cult of personality *(p.95)*.
- ✅ His control over the media and propaganda.
- ✅ The secret police, the NKVD *(p.89)*, and the Gulag *(p.90)* system system.

How did the purges help Stalin consolidate his power by 1941?

The purges helped Stalin consolidate his power in 5 main ways by:

- ✅ Removing all the 'Old Bolsheviks *(p.32)*' who had a personal connection to Lenin and who could potentially replace him as the leader by having them killed.
- ✅ Removing any potential threats in the army.
- ✅ Using terror to silence anyone likely to voice opposition to his policies in the media, sciences, arts and education.
- ✅ Using terror to ensure the compliance of the population.
- ✅ Using the secret police, NKVD *(p.89)*, and the gulag *(p.90)* system to remove anyone considered a possible threat from society.

How did Stalin's cult of personality help consolidate his power by 1941?

Stalin's *(p.121)* position was strengthened by his cult of personality *(p.95)* because it created a loyal following. Stalin was viewed as the father-figure of the USSR and in an almost god-like way.

Quizzes, amazing exam preparation tools and more at GCSEHistory.com

How did propaganda help consolidate Stalin's power by 1941?

The government of the USSR completely controlled all forms of information to which the population had access. This ensured the population was only exposed to the 'facts' and views the government wanted them to know. This reinforced Stalin's *(p.121)* cult of personality *(p.95)*.

 ## How did the secret police help consolidate Stalin's power by 1941?

The secret police and the gulag *(p.90)* system enabled Stalin *(p.121)* to consolidate his power by 1941 because it provided a method by which he could remove any opposition from all parts of in society.

 ## Why were there limits to how far Stalin could consolidate his power by 1941?

There were 6 key reasons why Stalin's consolidation of power by 1941 was limited or incomplete:

- ☑ The USSR was a difficult country to rule because it was so vast.
- ☑ It was difficult to control the far-flung regions as they did not always follow orders issued from Moscow.
- ☑ The central planning system was too inflexible and unresponsive to change.
- ☑ Managers often gave false data with regards to meeting targets and sacrificed quality to reach targets that were based on quantity. This undermined economic development.
- ☑ Bribery and corruption were very common at all levels in the Communist Party and the economy. This undermined the political and economic system.
- ☑ There were some instances of protests and disobedience against him despite his use of terror, particularly from the peasants against his collectivisation policy.

DID YOU KNOW?

Stalin had four children.

INDUSTRIALISATION

The aim of industrialisation was to transform the USSR into a modern industrialised nation.

 ## What was industrialisation?

Industrialisation was the process of accelerating the development of the Soviet Union to transform it from a backward country into a modern economy that could compete with the capitalist West.

 ## When did Stalin focus on industrialisation in the Soviet Union?

Stalin *(p.121)* focused on rapid industrialisation of the USSR happened between May 1929 and June 1941.

 ## Why did industrialisation happen in the USSR?

There were 6 main reasons why Stalin *(p.121)* wanted to industrialise the USSR:

- ☑ To prove himself to be the true successor of Lenin by continuing his work, and therefore, improving his own reputation as leader.
- ☑ By 1927, Stalin *(p.121)* feared the capitalist West would invade the USSR. The USSR needed to be able to modernise its army and mass produce weapons.
- ☑ According to Marxist theory, an advanced industrialised society was required for communism to flourish.

☑ The New Economic Policy seemed to have stalled as there was increasing unemployment, and in some areas of the economy the USSR had not yet reached the production levels of 1913.

☑ Politically, by changing his support from the NEP to rapid industrialisation, Stalin *(p.121)* was able to eliminate his opponents on the right of the Communist Party, such as Bukharin, in the leadership struggle.

☑ By introducing the Five Year Plans, he would increase his power and control over the USSR, as it would mean Moscow would have economic control over the whole of the country.

 ### How did the Soviet Union go through the process of industrialisation?

The USSR developed a command economy in which industrialisation was organised through central planning under the Five Year Plans. These 4 main steps were followed:

☑ The Communist Party set targets for production for the whole of the USSR.

☑ The Gosplan *(p.101)*, or the State Committee for Planning, transformed these overall targets to create targets for each different industry, such as coal or electricity, for each region of the country.

☑ Each region would then set targets for each factory, mine or workshop.

☑ Each factory would set targets for each foreman, who in turn set targets for individual workers.

 ### What were the successes of Soviet industrialisation?

Industrialisation under the Five Year Plans had 6 main successes:

☑ The USSR became more industrialised and was far more advanced in 1941 than it was in 1929, especially in heavy industry (coal, steel, iron, electricity).

☑ Transport improved with an increase in railways and canals.

☑ Industrial production levels increased dramatically from 1928 to 1939. For example, coal production increased from 35.5 million tons to 165.9 in 1940 - almost a fivefold increase.

☑ The USSR was able to fight Nazi Germany in the Second World War because industrialisation had created a modern weapons industry.

☑ The Five Year Plans helped create a larger working class as more industrial workers were needed in the cities and towns which led to people migrating from the countryside to the towns and cities. This would help develop a communist society.

☑ Despite the country being ruined in the struggle against the Nazis during the Second World War, the USSR still managed to beat the USA to almost all of the major milestones in the Space Race.

 ### What were the failures of Soviet industrialisation?

There were 8 key failures of the industrialisation and the Five Year Plans:

☑ The focus on heavy industry meant there were shortages in basic consumer goods, such as clothes and toiletries.

☑ Working conditions were often appalling and dangerous.

☑ Living conditions were awful and there was a shortage of housing.

☑ The goods produced were often of poor quality as targets were based on quantity.

☑ There was a lot of waste as the transport system wasn't efficient.

☑ Targets were not met and were often unrealistic. This led to unreasonable pressure on the factories; workers and managers could be jailed for failing to meet targets.

☑ It led to corruption, bribery and falsification of production figures.

☑ The system was not flexible. It could not react to changes in circumstances because everything was planned in advance.

 ### What was the outcome of industrialisation in USSR?

There were 4 main results of industrialisation.

☑ Heavy industry grew rapidly, and many industrial cities, such as Magnitogorsk, were built.

☑ Unemployment almost vanished.

☑ The USSR was able to re-arm and ultimately defeat Hitler in the Second World War.

☑ There were shortages of consumer goods.

 ## How were people affected by Soviet industrialisation?

Industrialisation had a massive impact on ordinary people in terms of bringing some benefit to their lives but mostly it had a negative impact.

 ## How did people benefit from Soviet industrialisation?

Industrialisation had 4 key benefits for ordinary people:

☑ Women had greater job opportunities. In 1927, only 28% of industrial workers were female. This increased to 40% by 1940.

☑ By the late 1930s, Soviet workers could get fairly well paid jobs and earn bonuses if they worked hard to meet their targets.

☑ Unemployment was incredibly low.

☑ Education was free and vocational education had been extended.

 ## How were people negatively impacted by Soviet industrialisation?

Industrialisation had 6 key negative consequences for ordinary people:

☑ Stalin's *(p.121)* priority was the industrialisation of the USSR. Therefore, the suffering of the ordinary people was of no consequence to him and was never dealt with.

☑ Internal passports were introduced to prevent workers from finding, and moving to, better jobs as this would disrupt production.

☑ Factory discipline and punishments were harsh. Workers faced fines, the threat of dismissal, or even arrest for not meeting targets.

☑ Housing was never a priority for Stalin *(p.121)*. As a result, overcrowding with poor facilities was a huge issue.

☑ Stalin's *(p.121)* focus on heavy industry in his Five Year Plans meant there was a constant shortage of consumer goods.

☑ Many of the workers on the massive engineering projects were gulag *(p.90)* prisoners; thousands died because of the terrible working conditions.

DID YOU KNOW?

Industrialisation was very successful in many ways because the USSR became a nuclear superpower.

However, the human cost was enormous.

FIVE YEAR PLANS

The Five Year Plans were blueprints of how the USSR would be transformed.

 ## What were the Five Year Plans?

The Five Year Plans were detailed economic plans drawn up to direct economic development. Each Five Year Plan was organised by Gosplan *(p.101)* and set targets for each industry by region, by factory and by individual workers. They were used to replace the New Economic Plan (NEP).

When were the Five Year Plans introduced?

The first Five Year Plan was started in 1928. Its focus was on developing heavy industry and collectivising agriculture.

Why replace the NEP with the Five Year Plan?

There were 4 main reasons why the NEP was replaced by the Five Year Plans:

- ☑ Stalin *(p. 121)* wanted to rapidly industrialise as he feared attack from the capitalist West.
- ☑ Economically, the NEP had created a few issues such as high unemployment and it had only brought production back to 1913 levels.
- ☑ Ideologically, the NEP was seen as too capitalist as it allowed small privately owned businesses to exist which created more successful peasants (Kulaks), traders and retailers called NEP men. The Five Year Plans would end this.
- ☑ Politically, it helped Stalin *(p. 121)* to remove his rival Bukharin during the leadership struggle because it isolated the right of Communist Party as it supported the NEP.

What were the successes of the Five Year Plans?

The greatest success of the Five Year Plans was that the USSR was industrialised and heavy industries such as coal, electricity and steel grew rapidly.

What were the failures of the Five Year Plans?

There were 3 key failures:

- ☑ Consumer goods were always neglected.
- ☑ Working and living conditions were awful.
- ☑ The targets that were set were never realistic and often not met.

What was the impact of the Five Year Plans on agriculture and the economy?

In farming, collectivisation was supposed to improve agricultural output. In reality, it led to starvation for millions in the Soviet Union. It was introduced so that excess grain could be sold abroad, with the profits used for industrialisation which was rapidly achieved.

What were the political aims of the Five Year Plans?

Stalin *(p. 121)* wanted the USSR to rapidly industrialise as he feared attack from the capitalist West and he wanted to control the rural areas. Ideologically, he was opposed to the idea of capitalism which he believed the NEP supported. Stalin believed in Marxist principles.

What were the Marxist principles Stalin applied to the Five Year Plan?

Stalin *(p. 121)* applied 5 Marxist principles to the Five Year Plan.

- ☑ Karl Marx believed that in a developed human society, countries would be industrialised.
- ☑ Factories should be made efficient and productive.
- ☑ There would be a steady move towards urbanisation.
- ☑ Fewer people would be needed to farm.
- ☑ Private property would be abolished and wealth would be redistributed to the poor.

What happened to the Five Year Plan after the war?

Stalin *(p. 121)* announced the Fourth Five Year Plan after the Second World War:

- ☑ Its aim was to concentrate on rebuilding the USSR after the Second World War and focused on heavy industry and technology. An example of this was by 1950 Ukraine's industrial output surpassing that of its pre-war levels.
- ☑ Again, consumer goods were not prioritised and failed to meet the targets set.

Quizzes, amazing exam preparation tools and more at GCSEHistory.com

GOSPLAN

The Gosplan was responsible for creating the Five Year Plans.

? What was the Gosplan?

Gosplan was the name for the 'State Committee for Planning', which was responsible for delivering the five year plans. Gosplan set targets for factory managers and workers and ensured they were achieved.

What was achieved by the Gosplan?

5,000 new factories were created between 1928 and 1937 under the planning and supervision of the Gosplan.

FIRST FIVE YEAR PLAN, 1928-32

The First Five Year Plan focused on developing the USSR as a modern, industrialised nation.

? What was the Soviet Union's First Five Year Plan?

The First Five Year Plan was the first industrial plan created by Gosplan *(p.101)* for the USSR.

When was the First Five Year Plan in the Soviet Union?

The First Five Year Plan was from October 1928 to December 1932.

What were the aims of the First 5 Year Plan in the Soviet Union?

The First Five Year Plan was focused on developing heavy industry such as steel, coal, iron and electricity. Approximately 80% of all investment went into heavy industry.

What were the successes of the First Five Year Plan in the Soviet Union?

The First Five Year Plan had 5 key successes:

- ☑ Electricity production trebled.
- ☑ The economy grew by 14% per year.
- ☑ Coal and iron output doubled and steel production increased by one-third.

✅ New industrial complexes were being built as well as machine tractor works.

✅ The targets were met in just four years, not five.

What were the weaknesses of the First Five Year Plan in the Soviet Union?

The First Five Year Plan had 5 key weaknesses:

✅ There was very little growth in consumer goods and fertilizers.

✅ The lack of skilled workers created instability, especially as many kept changing jobs.

✅ The quality of what was produced was low.

✅ Many targets were too high and not met, such as those in the chemical industry.

✅ Working and living conditions deteriorated further.

DID YOU KNOW?

In 1932, the British Embassy reported: 'Men, women, children, horses and other workers are left to die in order that the Five Year Plan shall at least succeed on paper.'

SECOND FIVE YEAR PLAN, 1933-37

The Second Five Year Plan did attempt to address some of the problems created by the First.

What was the Soviet Union's Second Five Year Plan?

The Second Five Year Plan was the second industrial plan created by Gosplan *(p.101)* for the USSR. It built on the work completed under the First Five Year Plan.

When was the Second Five Year Plan in the Soviet Union?

The Second Five Year Plan was from January 1933 to December 1937.

What were the aims of the Second Five Year Plan in the Soviet Union?

The 3 main aims of the Second Five Year Plan were:

✅ Still focused on developing heavy industry, but the targets were not so high.

✅ To develop communication.

✅ Higher targets for consumer goods to address the weaknesses of the First Five Year Plan.

What were the successes of the Second Five Year Plan in the Soviet Union?

The Second Five Year Plan had 5 main successes:

✅ By 1937, the USSR was self-sufficient in machine tool production and metal making.

✅ Transport and communications grew rapidly with the completion of such projects as the Moscow Metro.

✅ Chemical industries grew.

✅ Heavy industry benefitted from large scale projects being completed, such as Magnitogorsk Steel Plant and the Dnieper Dam.

✅ There were increases in heavy industry. For example, steel production increased four-fold.

What were the weaknesses of the Second Five Year Plan in the Soviet Union?

The Second Five Year Plan had 3 key weaknesses:

✅ There still was insufficient consumer goods and they failed to reach their targets.

✅ The Second Five Year Plan was disrupted due to the Great Purges.

✅ Oil production was poor.

DID YOU KNOW?

The White Sea Canal was one of the big projects constructed as a result of the Five Year Plans.

Many workers died building it. Unfortunately it was not a success because in some places it was too narrow and too shallow for the larger ships it was supposed to carry.

THIRD FIVE YEAR PLAN, 1938-41

The Third Five Year Plan was brought to end by the advent of the Second World War.

What was the Soviet Union's Third Five Year Plan?

The Third Five Year Plan was the third industrial plan created by Gosplan *(p. 101)* for the USSR. It built on the work completed under the Second Five Year Plan.

When was the Third Five Year Plan in the Soviet Union?

The Third Five Year Plan was from January 1938 to December 1941.

What were the aims of the Third Five Year Plan in the Soviet Union?

The Third Five Year Plan was still focused on developing heavy industry as there was a need for armaments to prepare for the Second World War.

What were the successes of the Third Five Year Plan in the Soviet Union?

The Third Five Year Plan had 2 main successes:

✅ Heavy industry grew.

✅ Defence and armaments grew quickly as one-third of investment was spent on them. This was the basis of a very strong armaments industry which was used during the Cold War.

What were the weaknesses of the Third Five Year Plan in the Soviet Union?

The Third Five Year Plan had 5 main weaknesses:

✅ The growth in steel output was poor.

✅ The plan was impacted by the Nazi Germany's invasion of the Soviet Union and it was ended early.

✅ The purges continued to impact the delivery of targets.

✅ Consumer good production suffered as resources had been diverted to the armaments industry.

✅ Oil production failed to meet its target and there was a fuel shortage.

THE STAKHANOVITE MOVEMENT

The Stakhanovite Movement inspired people to work even harder.

What was the Stakhanovite movement?

The Stakhanovite movement was the name given to workers that attempted to produce more than their targets, often by experimenting with new production techniques.

Who started the Stakhanovite movement?

Aleksei Stakhanov started the movement.

Why did Alexei Stakhanov start the Stakhanovite movement?

He was a coal miner who was extremely competitive and focused on ways to improve productivity.

What did Alexei Stakhanov do in the Stakhanovite movement?

Stakhanov did the following 4 main things:

- ☑ He and his team managed to mine 102 tons of coal in less than six hours - 14 times more than his quota on 30th August, 1935!
- ☑ He received a holiday, a new home and extra pay as a reward.
- ☑ He was held up by the Soviet Union as an example to other workers and became a national hero.
- ☑ He travelled the country as a celebrity and appeared on the cover of 'Time' magazine.

What were the results of the Stakhanovite movement?

There were 3 main results of the movement:

- ☑ It sometimes disrupted the otherwise smooth running of factories as Stakhanovites attempted to set new records for production.
- ☑ The Stakhanovite movement was used as propaganda.
- ☑ It encouraged workers to work harder as they were promised higher wages or more rations.

DID YOU KNOW?

George Orwell's famous allegorical novel, 'Animal Farm', represents the Stakhanovite movement through the character of a horse, called Boxer.

The horse's motto is: "I will work harder!'

COLLECTIVISATION, 1930S

Collectivisation fulfilled Stalin's economic and political goals.

What was collectivisation in the USSR?

Collectivisation was a policy of uniting small individual farms into larger collective farms. There were different types of collective farms. 'Kolkhozes' were farms where the peasants 'owned' the land, while 'Sovkhoz' were state-owned farms. This was enforced by the Soviet government in the late 1920s - early 1930s.

When was collectivisation introduced in the USSR?

Collectivisation was announced in 1927, encouraged by the government in 1928 and then enforced in 1929.

What happened to the peasants under Soviet collectivisation?

Under collectivisation, peasants were forced to share resources and work to government targets. Any profits left after state demands were met were shared equally among members of the collectives.

Why did Stalin bring in collectivisation in the USSR?

There were 7 important reasons why Stalin *(p.121)* brought in collectivisation:

- ☑ Ideologically, it would socialise the peasants and turn them into good communists by getting rid of private farms and removing class divisions by destroying the kulaks.
- ☑ Economically, collectivisation would fund industrialisation by increasing food production to feed the workers and to sell grain abroad.
- ☑ Collectivisation would enable farming to be mechanised which would free workers for the industrialisation process.
- ☑ Politically, collectivisation would increase the Communists Party's control over the countryside.
- ☑ Politically, it would enhance Stalin's *(p.121)* reputation in a similar way as the introduction of the Five Year Plans had.
- ☑ Politically, it would help Stalin *(p.121)* remove Bukharin as a rival in the leadership struggle as he favoured the NEP.
- ☑ Between 1927 and 1928, the government struggled to get enough grain to feed the workers in the towns because of the 'Scissors Crisis'. The peasants hoped that by reducing grain production it would push up prices. Collectivisation would stop this from happening.

How was collectivisation brought into the USSR?

There were 4 key ways in which collectivisation took place:

- ☑ Propaganda, force and terror were all used.
- ☑ Initially, voluntary collectivisation was tried, but failed as the peasants resisted it and killed their animals as well as the officials sent to collectivise them.
- ☑ In December 1929, Stalin *(p.121)* announced the 'liquidation of the kulaks as a class', also known as dekulakisation, and any peasant that opposed collectivisation was labelled a 'kulak *(p.107)*' and attacked.
- ☑ Stalin *(p.121)* enlisted an army of 25,000 party activists called the Twenty-Five Thousanders to force the collectivisation of the farms and to identify kulaks.

What were the consequences during collectivisation in the USSR for peasants who refused to collectivise?

The following happened to peasants that refused to cooperate:

- ☑ They were branded a 'kulak' *(p.107)*, and became targets for persecution.
- ☑ Around 30,000 kulaks were killed between 1930 and 1931.
- ☑ Up to 10 million were transported to labour camps in Siberia, where many were worked to death.

What were the initial problems with Soviet collectivisation?

Initially, there were 2 main problems with collectivisation:

☑ Both the richer and poorer peasants resented the government interfering in their lives.

☑ Peasants frequently destroyed their own crops and slaughtered their animals rather than hand them over to the communists.

 What were the key features of Kolkhozes, or collective farms, during collectivisation in the USSR?

The 5 key features of a Kolkhoz were:

☑ All land, tools and livestock were shared.

☑ The government decided what was grown, the hours worked and what jobs were to be done. The peasants were controlled so they could not leave the Kolkhoz.

☑ They consisted of 50 to 100 households.

☑ The government took most of the produce and paid very low prices so the farmers were paid very little.

☑ Families could have an acre of land to grow vegetables or keep animals.

 What was the role of machine tractor stations during collectivisation in the USSR?

Machine Tractor Stations, or MTS, were:

☑ Created so collective farms could rent machinery such as tractors.

☑ Created to control the peasants as they were run by the Communist Party.

☑ Used to oversee the collective farms to ensure compliance.

☑ Problematic. It was costly for the peasants to rent machinery as there wasn't enough of it and it was poorly maintained.

 What were the successes of Soviet collectivisation?

Collectivisation had 6 main successes:

☑ Farms were collectivised. In 1931, over 50% of households were collectivised. By the end of 1934, 70% of peasant households were in collectives. This increased to 90% by 1936.

☑ By the end of 1931, 22.8 million tonnes of grain had been collected. This was enough to feed the cities and export to fund industrialisation.

☑ It broke peasant resistance and destroyed the kulaks.

☑ It enabled rural areas to be turned communist.

☑ It meant the Communist Party extended its control over rural areas.

☑ There was enough machinery and changes in farming methods for peasants to be freed up so they could move to work in the new factories.

What were the failures of collectivisation in the USSR?

There were 4 main failures of collectivisation:

☑ Peasant opposition severely reduced production levels which took years to recover. Grain production did not exceed pre-collectivisation levels until 1935. Meat production did not return to pre-collectivisation levels until 1955.

☑ The USSR's agricultural technology did not improve.

☑ The machine tractor stations failed to deliver what was needed in terms of enough working machinery.

☑ The policy contributed to the Great Famine of 1932 - 1933. In the spring of 1932, a famine began in Ukraine and other areas (north Caucasus, Kazakhstan). By late 1934, approximately 7 million people had died.

How was collectivisation used to oppress Ukraine during collectivisation in the USSR?

Collectivisation was used to oppress Ukraine in 6 key ways:

- ✅ Ukraine, which was part of the Soviet Union, was a state with rich farmland.
- ✅ Lots of Ukrainians refused to join the collective farms. Those who resisted were brutally oppressed.
- ✅ Stalin *(p.121)* wanted to destroy Ukrainian nationalism and culture because of this opposition.
- ✅ The government increased the grain quotas, despite food production decreasing between 1932 and 1933.
- ✅ Officials took everything from the peasants when they could not meet the quotas.
- ✅ Thus, Ukraine suffered greatly during the Great Famine of 1932 - 1933, which is also called the 'Holodomor' - meaning 'death by hunger'.

How did collectivisation in the USSR contribute to the Great Famine?

Collectivisation made the Great Famine of 1932 - 1933 worse in 4 key ways:

- ✅ It severely disrupted farming which resulted in a decrease in production.
- ✅ The peasants resisted it by killing their animals and destroying their crops which meant there would be less food produced in subsequent years.
- ✅ The new collective farms were often badly run by the Twenty-Five Thousanders, who had little farming experience. This was the name given to workers from industrial cities who voluntarily left their homes to work on the frontline in rural areas.
- ✅ Many of the most experienced farmers were either deported, imprisoned in the gulags or executed.

DID YOU KNOW?

The forced collectivisation of the peasant farms was incredibly harsh.

Stalin was determined to break the peasants' resistance so they could not hold the government to ransom by withholding grain supplies and thus hinder industrialisation..

KULAKS

Kulaks were seen as enemies of the revolution.

Who were the kulaks?

Kulaks were peasants who were wealthy enough to own a farm and hire labour.

When were the kulaks attacked by the Communist government?

The kulaks were attacked by the Bolsheviks *(p.32)* at 3 different times:

- ✅ Between 1918 and 1921, the Bolsheviks *(p.32)* implemented their policy of War Communism. During this period, the kulaks were blamed for grain shortages as peasants resisted grain requisitioning.
- ✅ Between 1921 and 1928, the communists implemented their NEP. During this time, the kulaks were accused of being capitalists and against the revolution as they became richer.
- ✅ Between 1928 and 1932, the communists implemented collectivisation. The kulaks were accused of being capitalists and 'class enemies', and Stalin *(p.121)* launched a dekulakisation campaign.

Why were kulaks considered anti-communist?

The kulaks were considered anti-Communist due to 3 main reasons:

✅ They strongly opposed collectivisation as they wanted to own their farms.

✅ They didn't want to sell their grain to the government because purchasing prices were low.

✅ The Soviet government considered the kulaks to be capitalists and, therefore, enemies of communism.

 What happened to the kulaks?

Kulaks were considered enemies of communism and most ended up in one of 3 categories during collectivisation:

✅ 'Counter-revolutionaries', who were to be shot or sent to the gulags.

✅ 'Active opponents of collectivisation', who were deported to other areas of the USSR.

✅ Those who were expelled from farms and forced to settle on poor land.

 What was the impact of collectivisation on the kulaks?

Collectivisation destroyed the kulaks as a class and many were exiled, imprisoned in gulags, or executed.

> ### DID YOU KNOW?
> ---
> Stalin said in 1929: 'Now we are able to carry on a determined offensive against the kulaks, to break their resistance, to eliminate them as a class.'

LIVING IN TOWNS AND THE COUNTRYSIDE, 1924-41

Living conditions in the USSR were harsh as they were not prioritised by the government.

 What were living conditions like in the Soviet Union?

Living conditions in the Soviet Union varied hugely. It depended on where you lived and who you were.

 What were the living conditions in the Soviet Union countryside like?

In the countryside the living conditions were poor in 4 main ways:

✅ There was only basic housing, with outside toilets and no running water.

✅ Peasants were not allowed to leave their farms and had passports for internal travel.

✅ There was rationing, which allowed Stalin *(p. 121)* to confiscate excess food for distribution in the cities.

✅ The peasants received less food than the workers in the towns and cities and so had to travel to buy food.

 What were the living conditions like in the Soviet Union towns?

In the towns the living conditions were poor in 8 main ways:

✅ There was insufficient housing in towns and cities because industrialisation led to a rapid increase in the number of workers.

✅ Housing was of low quality and living standards were poor.

✅ Most lived communally, with several families sharing one apartment. Each family had one room for their whole family to live, but shared the kitchen and bathroom.

✅ Some people were 'corner dwellers' as they lived in a shed, a cupboard or, literally, the corner of a corridor.

- ☑ Food was not plentiful - queuing for food was a common occurrence in the Soviet Union during the 1930s. Food rationing was introduced between 1929 and 1935.
- ☑ There were shortages in everyday consumer goods such as toiletries and clothes.
- ☑ There were long queues for consumer goods when they were available.
- ☑ The Second World War made the situation worse as approximately 1/3 of urban housing was damaged or destroyed.

 What did the government do to improve living conditions in towns in the Soviet Union?

The government tried to improve the towns and cities by providing leisure activities such as cinemas, parks and various sporting facilities.

 What were the living conditions like in the new factory towns in the Soviet Union?

The living conditions in the new factory towns created by industrialisation were awful in 4 main ways:

- ☑ Many people lived in barracks or other forms of communal accommodation with not enough furniture.
- ☑ Sanitation was inadequate with insufficient washing facilities, running water or toilets. Disease thus spread quickly, leading to high sickness rates.
- ☑ There was little infrastructure such as proper roads, sewers or electricity.
- ☑ Living conditions were very slow to improve during the 1930s.

 What were the living conditions of the party officials of the Soviet Union?

The living conditions for the party officials were very good in 2 main ways:

- ☑ Party officials lived in relative luxury, compared to ordinary people in the USSR. Their accommodation was larger and not communal.
- ☑ They had access to special shops where they could buy consumer goods as a reward for their loyalty, and access to more and better quality food.

DID YOU KNOW?

Housing was never prioritised by Stalin, even after the destruction caused by the Second World War.

It was only after Stalin's death in 1953 that massive housing projects were developed to meet demand.

WORKING IN TOWNS AND THE COUNTRYSIDE, 1924-41

Working conditions could be terrible in the USSR as health and safety was neglected.

 What were working conditions like in the towns and countryside in the Soviet Union?

The working conditions in the towns and countryside in the Soviet Union were poor and often dangerous.

 What were working conditions like in the towns in the Soviet Union?

Working conditions in the towns were difficult and it was very physically demanding in 5 main ways:

- ☑ Trade unions could not protect the workers from the poor working conditions or low pay because they had little power.
- ☑ Working conditions were dangerous. There were many accidents because health and safety was considered irrelevant.

- To encourage workers to work harder, piecework was introduced - people were paid by how much they produced. This meant working harder to increase wages.
- Workers did not have the right to leave their job to look for another one because of the internal passports.
- Stalin *(p.121)* brought in an incredibly harsh labour code in 1940, which set out harsh punishments for lateness with pay cuts, arrest for changing jobs without permission, and an increase in the hours and the number of days workers had to work.

What were working conditions like in the countryside in the Soviet Union?

The working conditions in the countryside on the collective farms were poor in 3 main ways:

- The pay was terrible and much lower than in the factories.
- It was very restrictive. They were told what to plant and when, and could not leave the collective farms without permission.
- The work was very physically demanding with long hours as there was a lack of machinery at the machine tractor stations.

What were the positives of the working conditions in the Soviet Union?

There were 4 main benefits to working:

- There was full employment, even if the jobs were terrible.
- The factories had canteens which provided relatively cheap food.
- Women with children could access childcare facilities in towns.
- Shock brigades, or workers who exceeded production targets, could earn more.

DID YOU KNOW?

At the time of the Bolshevik Revolution, less than one-sixth of the population of Russia were industrial workers.

FAMILY LIFE, 1924-41

The USSR's social policies aimed to create a specific type of family that served the needs of the nation.

What was the Soviet Union's view on family?

The Soviet Union's view on the family changed over time, from a period of more experimentation in the 1920s to Stalin's *(p.121)* Great Retreat *(p.111)* in 1936 which promoted traditional family values.

What were the Soviet Union views on homosexuality and family?

The USSR's views on homosexuality changed over time in 3 key ways:

- When the new communist government rewrote the Criminal Codes in 1922 and 1926, they did not include any law which prohibited homosexuality, so it was therefore legal.
- Attitudes tended to be homophobic and homosexuals suffered verbal and physical abuse.
- Stalin's *(p.121)* government made homosexuality illegal again in 1933.

What was the Soviet Union view on abortion and family?

The USSR's attitude to abortion changed over time in 4 main ways.

- ✅ Abortion was made legal in 1917.
- ✅ Abortions were made illegal in 1936 in a bid to boost population growth and ensure the next generation of workers.
- ✅ Many women resorted to illegal, unregulated abortions as a result.
- ✅ Contraceptives were hard to obtain.

What was the Soviet Union's view on working women and family?

Women were encouraged to work:

- ✅ There were 3 million women workers in the Soviet Union in 1928.
- ✅ This number had risen to more than 13 million by 1940.
- ✅ While around 40% of industrial workers were women, according to available figures, this still meant the majority of those employed in heavy industry were male.

How did Stalin's Great Retreat impact the family in the Soviet Union?

Stalin's *(p. 121)* Great Retreat *(p. 111)* in 1936, promoted traditional family values in 3 main ways:

- ✅ Encouraging families to have children by offering financial rewards.
- ✅ Making abortion illegal.
- ✅ Making divorce more difficult and expensive. Stalin *(p. 121)* believed marriage breakdown had led to abandoned children roaming the streets.

DID YOU KNOW?

Women bore the brunt of the consequences of the Soviet Union's social policies.

Theirs was a 'double burden'; they often held both full-time jobs and had responsibility for the home.

STALIN'S GREAT RETREAT

The Great Retreat was a period of time in which social policies pushed a traditional agenda.

What was the Great Retreat?

The Great Retreat was a policy introduced by Stalin *(p. 121)* in the USSR which promoted traditional family values.

When was the Great Retreat?

The Great Retreat occurred during the 1930s.

Why did Stalin introduce the Great Retreat?

The Great Retreat of the 1930s was introduced because due to 4 main reasons:

- ✅ It was a reaction to the perceived failures of the government's policies on the family and women of the 1920s.
- ✅ The birth rate had dropped.
- ✅ Family breakdown had increased causing social problems.
- ✅ It was felt that there was a breakdown in discipline in education and of the youth.

 ## How did the Great Retreat affect families?

There were 5 key changes that affected family life because of the Great Retreat:

- ✅ Parents could be fined if their child was in trouble with the authorities.
- ✅ Divorce was discouraged by increasing the cost from 4 to 50 roubles and forcing couples to attend court.
- ✅ Divorced fathers had to pay child maintenance. If they did not pay they could be jailed for up to two years.
- ✅ Male homosexuality was made illegal.
- ✅ Abortion was made illegal to encourage larger families.

 ## How did the Great Retreat affect education?

In the Great Retreat, Stalin *(p.121)* re-introduced exams, homework, traditional teaching methods and subjects, and textbooks set by the government. School became much more strict as tighter discipline was re-introduced.

 ## What was the impact of the Great Retreat?

The Great Retreat had 3 main effects:

- ✅ It had a negative effect on women. It promoted traditional family values which restricted many of the new opportunities women had in the 1920s.
- ✅ The birth rate increased temporarily.
- ✅ The divorce rate decreased.

DID YOU KNOW?

The USSR in the 1920s witnessed some social experimentation in terms of society and culture.

However, there was always tension with the traditional views of some Communist Party members and society in general.

ETHNIC GROUPS

The Soviet Union's treatment of ethnic groups was harsh.

 ## What was the persecution of ethnic minorities in the Soviet Union?

Ethnic minorities were treated as a potential threat to Stalin's *(p.121)* position and the communist government. Therefore, they were persecuted and were treated with hostility.

 ## When did the persecution of ethnic minorities in the USSR take place?

The persecution of ethnic minorities increased in the 1930s and continued until Stalin's *(p.121)* death in 1953.

 ## Why did the persecution of ethnic minorities in the USSR take place?

There were 3 main reasons why ethnic minorities were persecuted:

- ✅ The USSR was made up of many different nationalities. Many of these had distinct identities and wanted independence from the Soviet Union. They were therefore seen as a threat to unity.
- ✅ Stalin *(p.121)* blamed specific nationalities for the resistance to collectivisation. Some believe that is why he failed to help the Ukrainians during the famine of 1932.

Stalin *(p.121)* believed that because some nationalities wanted independence, they could not be trusted when the Soviet Union was under threat of invasion or at war.

What happened to ethnic minorities in the USSR during the persecution?

There were 6 different ways in which ethnic minorities were persecuted:

☑ All 15 republics of the USSR had to suppress their local culture and language.

☑ All schools had to teach Russian *(p.76)* and loyalty to the USSR.

☑ During the purges between 1936 and 1938, many national leaders, teachers and writers were arrested and either executed or imprisoned in the gulags.

☑ Whole national groups were moved or deported to different areas in the USSR. For example, when Nazi Germany invaded in 1941, all Germans in the Volga area were rounded up and exiled to either central Asia or Siberia.

☑ The Second World War led to an increase in purges of ethnic groups during the war, and after it had ended, as Stalin *(p.121)* became increasingly paranoid. For example, there were mass deportations of Lithuanians, Estonians and Latvians.

☑ The last major attack on an ethnic group was the Mingrelian Affair in 1951, in which a purge began in Georgia aimed at the leader of the NKVD *(p.89)*, Lavrentiy Beria, who was also Mingrelian.

DID YOU KNOW?

One example of resistance was in the Turkestan region, by a Muslim group called the Basmachi. It took the Soviet Army 8 years to crush their rebellion.

TSARINA ALEXANDRA

'Be more autocratic than Peter the Great and sterner than Ivan the Terrible.' - Tsarina Alexandra to her husband, Tsar Nicholas II, in 1895

Who was Tsarina Alexandra?

Alexandra Feodorovna was a German Princess who married Tsar Nicholas II *(p.20)* in 1894. She was unpopular at court.

What was Tsarina Alexandra famous for?

Tsarina Alexandra was famous for 4 key reasons:

☑ She was disliked at court, partly because she was German and Russia was at war with Germany during the First World War.

☑ When Nicholas II took personal command of the Russian Army in August 1915, he left Alexandra in charge of the government as his regent. She did a terrible job. She sacked capable ministers and replaced them with incompetent men.

☑ She allowed Rasputin to have too much influence over the running of the country.

☑ Her actions helped to increase opposition to tsarist rule, which in turn led to the February Revolution *(p.47)* 1917.

What was Tsarina Alexandra's relationship with Rasputin?

Tsarina Alexandra had a close relationship with Rasputin:

☑ She believed that Rasputin had mystical healing powers and could help her son, Alexei, who suffered from haemophilia.

- Rasputin had a great deal of influence over Tsarina Alexandra. Nicholas II made her regent in August 1915 because he had taken over personal command of the Russian Army during the First World War. Rasputin interfered with the appointments of ministers.
- There were rumours that Rasputin and Tsarina Alexandra were having an affair.

 When did Tsarina Alexandra die?

Tsarina Alexandra and her family were executed by the Bolsheviks *(p.32)* on 17th July 1918, during the Russian Civil War *(p.65)*, to prevent the Whites and the Czech Legion from rescuing them.

DID YOU KNOW?

3 facts about Tsarina Alexandra:
- ✔ She was a German princess and granddaughter of Queen Victoria.
- ✔ Her marriage to Nicholas was based on love.
- ✔ She had 5 children.

LEV KAMENEV

Lev Kamenev was considered a rival by Stalin.

 Who was Kamenev?

Lev Kamenev was from a working class family. He joined the Bolshevik *(p.32)* Party and became a leading member of the Party. He became a close friend of Lenin and spent time with him in exile.

 When did Kamenev join the Communist Party?

Kamenev joined the Bolshevik *(p.32)* Party in 1903.

 What was Lenin's relationship with Kamenev?

Kamenev was a close friend of Lenin's, but had opposed his plan for a revolution in October 1917.

 What were Kamenev's political beliefs?

Kamenev was on the left of the Communist Party. He believed in permanent or world-wide revolution and was against the New Economic Policy, NEP *(p.73)*.

 What did Lenin say about Kamenev in his 'Testament'?

Lenin criticised Kamenev for not supporting him in the October Revolution *(p.56)* of 1917 in his 'Testament'.

 What roles did Kamenev have in the Communist Party?

Kamenev held 4 key positions of responsibility:

- He was in charge of the Communist Party in Petrograd when he returned from exile in March 1917.
- In 1919, he became the leader of the Communist Party in Moscow.
- Between March 1921 and 1926, he was a full member of the Politburo *(p.71)*.
- When Lenin died in 1924, he was the acting head of the communist government.

What happened to Kamenev during the leadership struggle with Stalin?

In 1925, Stalin *(p.121)* allied with Kamenev and Zinoviev to defeat Trotsky. Between 1927 and 1929 Stalin turned against Kamenev and allied with Bukharin.

What happened to Kamenev in the Great Purges?

Stalin *(p.121)* viewed Kamenev as a threat so was targeted in the Great Purges of 1936 to 1938:

- ☑ He was arrested and put on trial during the Trial of the Sixteen in 1936 with Zinoviev.
- ☑ He was accused of the murder of Kirov, plotting to overthrow the government and sabotaging the Five Year Plans.
- ☑ Kamenev confessed to the crimes of which he was accused to save the lives of his family. He was executed by being shot.

When did Kamenev die?

Kamenev was executed after his show trial on 24th August, 1936. He was shot.

DID YOU KNOW?

3 facts about Kamenev:
- ✔ He did not finish his university education because he was thrown out as he demonstrated against the tsar.
- ✔ He was married to Leon Trotsky's sister, Olga, and they had two children.
- ✔ Although he confessed to save his family, his wife and sons were shot.

ALEXANDER KERENSKY

Alexander Kerensky was the second leader of the Provisional Government.

Who was Alexander Kerensky?

Alexander Kerensky was a member of the Socialist Revolutionary Party *(p.30)* in Russia and of the Provisional Government *(p.50)* between March 1917 and October 1917.

When was Alexander Kerensky important?

Kerensky became important between March 1917 and October 1917.

Why was Alexander Kerensky important?

Kerensky was important for 7 key reasons:

- ☑ He investigated the Lena Goldfield Massacre of 1912.
- ☑ He was elected as a member of the fourth Duma *(p.39)* as a delegate from the Trudovik Party. This was a party formed when some members of the Socialist Revolutionary Party *(p.30)* broke away because of the Party's decision to not take part in the first Duma *(p.37)*.
- ☑ He was appointed vice-chairman of the Petrograd Soviet *(p.49)*.
- ☑ He was made the Minister of War in May 1917, and organised the failed June Offensive *(p.52)* against Germany and Austria, which led to the July Days unrest.
- ☑ He appointed General Kornilov as the commander-in-chief of the Russian Army and had to use the Bolsheviks *(p.32)* to stop General Kornilov's attempted revolt in July 1917.

☑ He became the leader of the Provisional Government *(p.50)* in July 1917.

☑ He failed to stop the Bolsheviks *(p.32)* from overthrowing the Provisional Government *(p.50)* in October 1917.

 When did Alexander Kerensky die?

Kerensky fled to America from Russia after the October Revolution *(p.56)* of 1917 and lived there until his death in 1970.

DID YOU KNOW?

Kerensky's father taught Lenin at school.

SERGEI KIROV

Stalin saw Sergei Kirov as a threat to his position as Party leader.

 Who was Kirov?

Sergei Kirov joined the Communist Party in 1904 and participated in the 1905 Revolution, the October 1917 Revolution and the Civil War. He became a leading member of the Communist Party and the government of the Soviet Union in the 1930s.

 What roles did Kirov have in the Communist Party?

Kirov held 3 key positions of responsibility in the Communist Party and the government of the USSR:

☑ In 1921, he was appointed the head of the Azerbaijan Communist Party.

☑ In 1926, Kirov was appointed as the head of the Leningrad Communist Party.

☑ Kirov was a member of the Politburo *(p.71)* from July 1930 to his death in 1934.

 Why did Kirov's relationship with Stalin deteriorate?

Kirov's relationship with Stalin *(p.121)* deteriorated for 5 main reasons:

☑ Kirov was popular and charismatic so Stalin *(p.121)* saw him as an opponent.

☑ In 1932, Kirov voted with others in the Politburo *(p.71)* against the execution of Ryutin. Ryutin had criticised Stalin's *(p.121)* policies of industrialisation and collectivisation in a 200 page article .

☑ During the 17th Party Congress, Kirov was given a standing ovation that was longer than the applause for Stalin *(p.121)*.

☑ During the 17th Party Congress, Kirov made critical comments about the effects of industrialisation and collectivisation.

☑ He received more votes than Stalin *(p.121)* for a position on the Central Committee.

 When was Kirov murdered?

Kirov was assassinated by being shot in the back of the neck on 1st December, 1934 by Leonid Nikolayev.

 Why was Kirov's murder significant?

Kirov was significant due to 3 key reasons:

☑ He challenged Stalin's *(p.121)* position of power as shown by events during the 17th Party Congress.

☑ Stalin *(p.121)* realised that he was not completely secure in his position as leader.

☑ It is likely that Stalin *(p.121)* organised the assassination of Kirov as an excuse to begin the purges.

> **DID YOU KNOW?**
>
> **Sergei Kirov's murder was very suspicious.**
> Leonid Nikolayev, his assassin, managed to slip past the guards of the Smolny Institute where Kirov worked and shoot him in the corridor.

GENERAL KORNILOV

General Kornilov was an experienced officer in both the Russo-Japanese War and the First World War.

Who was General Kornilov?

General Lavr Kornilov was a capable Russian general who served under the tsar *(p.19)* and the Provisional Government *(p.50)* during the First World War.

When was General Kornilov appointed to his role?

General Kornilov was appointed as commander-in-chief of Russian forces by the Provisional Government *(p.50)* in July 1917.

Why was General Kornilov appointed?

General Kornilov was appointed commander-in-chief to improve army discipline so Russia could win the First World War.

What was the role of General Kornilov?

General Kornilov had 3 main roles in the First World War:

☑ He was ruthless and opposed the Petrograd Soviet *(p.49)* and left-wing groups.

☑ He was suspected of trying to overthrow the Provisional Government *(p.50)* in July 1917 after he was ordered to bring troops to Petrograd to deal with the July uprising. This was known as the Kornilov affair.

☑ General Kornilov was sacked and the Provisional Government *(p.50)* lost the support of the army.

What were the results of General Kornilov's actions?

There were 2 main results of General Kornilov's actions in the Kornilov Affair:

☑ The Provisional Government *(p.50)* gave weapons to the Petrograd Soviet *(p.49)* to arm the Bolsheviks *(p.32)* to defend Petrograd against General Kornilov.

☑ He was arrested on 1st September, 1917.

How did General Kornilov die?

General Kornilov escaped and fought with the Whites during the civil war, in which he died.

DID YOU KNOW?

3 facts about General Kornilov:
- ✔ He believed in very strict military discipline and wanted to bring back capital punishment.
- ✔ He was very conservative.
- ✔ He died in a shell explosion in Ekaterinodar.

VLADIMIR LENIN

Lenin was the USSR's first leader as well as its founder.

Who was Lenin?

Lenin was the leader of the Russian Communist Party and the USSR. He developed the political theory of Marxism-Leninism. His full name was Vladimir Ilyich Ulyanov.

When did Lenin join the Communist Party?

Lenin joined the Communist Party in 1903 and became the leader of the USSR after the October Revolution *(p.56)* of 1917 until his death in 1924.

Where was Lenin during the February Revolution?

Lenin was in exile in Switzerland. This meant he did not play a part in the February Revolution *(p.47)*.

When did Lenin return to Russia?

Lenin returned to Russia on 3rd April, 1917 but fled to Finland in July 1917. He returned again on 10th October, 1917.

Why did Lenin return to Russia?

Lenin was helped by the Germans to return to Russia. The Germans wanted to cause unrest in Russia in the hope the country would pull out of the First World War. They believed Lenin would cause that unrest.

What were Lenin's April theses?

Lenin's manifesto, his 'April Theses' had 4 main demands.
- ☑ Peace: He demanded that Russia pull out of the war.
- ☑ Bread: Lenin claimed the Bolsheviks *(p.32)* could solve the food shortages.
- ☑ Land: Lenin wanted land to be given to the peasants and to end the social hierarchies that had existed under the tsar. *(p.19)*
- ☑ All power to the Soviets: Lenin demanded all cooperation with the Provisional Government *(p.50)* and any other party should end, and all power should be with the Soviets.

What was Lenin's 'State and Revolution' pamphlet about?

The 'State and Revolution' pamphlet was:
- ☑ Written by Lenin while he was in Finland.

- ☑ Stated that after taking power in a revolution, there would be a period of rule known as the ' dictatorship of the proletariat'.
- ☑ Its aim would be to create stability in the nation before the transition to full communism.

What part did Lenin play in the Sovnarkom?

Lenin did the following on the Sovnarkom *(p.70)*, or the Council of People's Commissars:

- ☑ He was its chairman.
- ☑ He used the Sovnarkom *(p.70)* to develop a dictatorship, rather than Russia becoming a genuinely equal socialist society.

When did Lenin die?

Lenin died on 21st January 1924 after suffering three strokes; the first in May 1922, the second in December 1922 and the final one in March 1923.

Who were Lenin's potential successors?

After Lenin's death in 1924, there was a power struggle over who would succeed him:

- ☑ There were several potential leaders - Stalin *(p.121)*, Trotsky, Kamenev, Zinoviev and Bukharin.
- ☑ Each candidate had their own strengths: Stalin *(p.121)* was general secretary of the Communist Party, Trotsky had led the Red Army, and Zinoviev and Kamenev had led the party in Petrograd and Moscow.

Who succeeded Lenin?

By 1929, Stalin *(p.121)* emerged as leader of the Communist Party and of the country.

How did Lenin's successor become leader?

There were 2 main methods Stalin *(p.121)* used to become Lenin's successor:

- ☑ He manipulated his rivals, who were also competing to become leader of the party, so he was able to remove them as competitors.
- ☑ He appeared to be the most moderate candidate and rose above the arguments and egos of his rivals.

What were Lenin's achievements?

Lenin was the communist leader of Russia and the USSR between 1917 and 1924. He achieved 7 important things:

- ☑ He adapted Karl Marx's theory of communism to create Marxism-Leninism. This was a theory on how to achieve a communist society in Russia in a shorter period of time than Marxism would allow.
- ☑ He created the 'April Theses' which enabled the Bolsheviks *(p.32)* to get their message across more easily and gained them more support.
- ☑ He had led a successful communist revolution in Russia in October 1917.
- ☑ He led the Bolsheviks *(p.32)* to victory in the Russian Civil War *(p.65)*.
- ☑ He introduced War Communism which centralised Bolshevik *(p.32)* control of the economy, increased centralisation of the party and enabled them win the civil war.
- ☑ He ended Russia's war with Germany through the Treaty of Brest-Litovsk *(p.63)* in March 1918.
- ☑ He created a one-party state or a dictatorship.

PRINCE LVOV

Prince Lvov was the head of the Provisional Government.

Who was Prince Lvov?

Prince Lvov was an aristocrat who was a liberal and Russian social reformer. He joined the Constitutional Democratic (Kadet) Party *(p.31)* in 1905 and was elected to the first Duma *(p.37)*. He became the first leader of the Provisional Government *(p.50)*.

When was Prince Lvov the leader of the Provisional Government?

Prince Lvov was the leader of the Provisional Government *(p.50)* between March and July 1917.

What did Prince Lvov do as leader of the Provisional Government?

As leader of the Provisional Government *(p.50)*, Prince Lvov continued with the war against Germany and had to resign after the July Days unrest.

GRIGORI RASPUTIN

'He is just a good, religious, simple-minded Russian. When in trouble or assailed by doubts, I like to have a talk with him, and I invariably feel at peace with myself afterward.' - Tsar Nicholas II speaking about Rasputin in 1905

Who was Rasputin?

Grigori Rasputin was a Russian mystic who claimed he had healing powers. Some people thought he was a charlatan, but he became very powerful at the court of Tsar Nicholas II *(p.20)*.

When was Rasputin born?

Rasputin was born on 21st January, 1869.

How did Rasputin make it to the court?

Rasputin became a wanderer after he had a holy experience. He eventually found his way to the court of Nicholas II because he had a reputation as a healer.

What was Rasputin's role in the court?

Rasputin first became a healer for Alexei, son of Nicholas II and his wife, who had haemophilia. He also advised Tsarina Alexandra *(p.113)*.

Why was Rasputin controversial?

There were 4 key reasons why Rasputin was considered controversial:

- ☑ He started to accept bribes and sexual favours.
- ☑ Many believed he had an affair with Alexandra, the tsarina.
- ☑ Rasputin advised Alexandra over appointments to the government and interfered with political decisions during the First World War while the tsar *(p.19)* was at the frontline. People questioned how effective the government was, and how much influence Rasputin's had.
- ☑ The Tsarina would not listen to any criticism of Rasputin.

When was Rasputin murdered?

Rasputin was murdered in December 1916, by a group of aristocrats.

Why was Rasputin murdered?

Rasputin was murdered because he was hated by many members of the aristocracy as he was ruining the reputation of the royal family.

DID YOU KNOW?

Rasputin was assassinated.

He was poisoned, shot and then drowned because his influence over Tsarina Alexandra played an important role in damaging the royal family's reputation.

JOSEPH STALIN

Joseph Stalin was the brutal dictator of the USSR from 1929 to 1953.

Who was Joseph Stalin?

Joseph Stalin was a communist revolutionary from Georgia who was a member of the Communist Party and became the leader of the Soviet Union.

When did Stalin join the Communist Party?

Stalin joined the Communist Party in 1903. He was the leader of the USSR from the mid-1920s until his death in 1953.

What was Stalin's role in the Communist Party?

Stalin had 3 main positions in the Communist Party:

☑ In January 1912, Stalin was a member of the first Central Committee of the Bolshevik *(p.32)* Party.

☑ He became the Commissar for Nationalities between 1917 and 1923 and was appointed the Commissar for State Control from 1919 to 1923.

☑ In 1922, Stalin was appointed the general secretary of the party's Central Committee.

Why was Stalin able to become the leader of the USSR?

There were 5 main reasons why Stalin became the leader of the USSR:

☑ He was a very clever politician who exploited the weaknesses of his rivals.

☑ His policies, such as socialism in one country, were more popular than Trotsky's policies.

☑ He used his power within the Communist Party as general secretary to put his own supporters into important posts to build his own power base.

☑ He turned circumstances to his advantage, such as using Lenin's funeral to undermine Trotsky.

☑ He played his rivals against one another so they undermined each other.

What happened during the purges under Stalin?

Stalin initiated 3 main purges at different times:

☑ The Great Purge occurred between 1936 and 1938. Old Bolsheviks *(p.32)* and all those suspected of being an 'enemy of the people' were targeted. Essentially, this meant anyone who posed a threat to Stalin, real or imagined.

☑ During the Second World War, different nationalities were targeted, such as the Volga Germans and ethnic Finns, as their loyalty was considered suspect.

☑ After the Second World War, different groups such as Jews, Russian soldiers who had been German prisoners of war and the Leningrad Communist Party were purged.

What was Stalin's influence on education?

Stalin influenced education in three specific ways:

☑ The government decided what the school curriculum would be and what subjects would be taught. All schools taught sciences, Russian and communist ideology.

☑ The textbooks had to be approved by the government and must contain the 'correct' facts.

☑ The new textbooks rewrote history and praised Stalin as Lenin's loyal follower. The core curriculum was shaped according to Stalin's world view with the aim of creating new 'Soviet men' and 'Soviet women'.

How did art and culture in the Soviet Union develop under Stalin's rule?

Art and culture was controlled by the Soviet government in 3 key ways:

☑ The government had complete control over information and propaganda through the Commissariat of Enlightenment. This included all art and culture.

☑ Socialist realism *(p.93)* was the regime's official art form. Its artists included Kuzma Petrov-Vodkin, Isaak Brodsky, Alexander Samokhvalov and Yuri Pimenov.

☑ Socialist realist art work was easy to understand and focused on workers in everyday situations. These workers were depicted as the heroes of Soviet society. The same rules applied to novels and music.

What was Stalin's view on Christianity?

The communists, as atheists, opposed the Russian Orthodox Church. Many churches were shut down and their priests imprisoned and even shot. Only 500 churches remained open by 1941, a reduction of almost 50,000 since the beginning of the First World War.

How did Stalin's regime treat Muslims?

Stalin oppressed Muslims using 4 main strategies:

- ☑ The use of Arabic writing was frowned upon and many non-Russian speakers were 're-educated' to speak Russian.
- ☑ Muslim schools and places of worship were closed down.
- ☑ Participating in the Hajj pilgrimage to Mecca was forbidden.
- ☑ The Soviet government organised unveiling of women campaigns.

How did Stalin's regime treat Judaism?

With regard to Judaism, anti-Semitism was illegal but many religious Jews were discriminated against. Stalin wanted to move all Jews to a designated region in the east called the Jewish Autonomous Oblast, but this idea failed.

Was the media censored under Stalin's regime?

The media had to be supportive of Stalin and the Communist Party. Works written by those who had been purged were banned, including Trotsky's. Economic data was also censored, which meant no one could check the claims of the government about the economy.

What were Joseph Stalin's beliefs?

Stalin believed in one-party rule. He was also convinced that the West wanted to destroy communism.

What conferences did Stalin attend?

Stalin attended the Tehran, Yalta and Potsdam conferences, which were discussions on Nazi Germany and how to end the war.

What was Stalin's involvement in the Cold War?

Stalin did not trust the West. His poor relationship with President Truman especially led to a deterioration in US-Soviet relations.

When did Stalin die?

Stalin died of a stroke on 5th March, 1953.

DID YOU KNOW?

3 facts about Stalin:

- ✔ His alias, Stalin, meant 'Man of Steel.'
- ✔ He committed bank robberies to help fund communist activities.
- ✔ He was sent to a seminary as a teenager to study as priest.

LEON TROTSKY

Leon Trotsky was the architect of the Red Army's success in the Russian Civil War.

Who was Trotsky?

Leon Trotsky was a Soviet revolutionary, Marxist theorist, and politician. Trotsky was a brilliant orator - he was much more charismatic than Stalin *(p.121)*. He had worked closely with Lenin as the war commissar, commander of the Red Army.

Where was Trotsky during the February Revolution?

Trotsky had been in the USA during the February Revolution *(p.47)*. In May 1917, after the February Revolution, he returned to Russia.

What did Trotsky believe in?

Trotsky believed in 'permanent revolution'. His argument was that the revolution would degenerate if it could not spread and become international. He thought the Bolsheviks *(p.32)* should use instability around the world to spark revolutions elsewhere. This brought him into conflict with Stalin *(p.121)*. Stalin believed in 'Socialism in One Country'.

What were Trotsky's main roles?

Trotsky had 4 key roles:

- ☑ He was elected president of the Petrograd Soviet *(p.49)* on 25th September 1917, because the Bolsheviks *(p.32)* had protected Petrograd from the Kornilov Revolt *(p.54)*.
- ☑ Trotsky played a key role in the October Revolution *(p.56)* in 1917, where he used the Military Revolutionary Committee to take over road bridges, telegraph offices and the army headquarters.
- ☑ Trotsky's was appointed as Commissar for War during the Russian Civil War *(p.65)*. In this role, he was responsible for the Red Army, and his actions were one of the key reasons the Bolsheviks *(p.32)* won.
- ☑ Trotsky negotiated the Treaty of Brest-Litovsk *(p.63)* with Germany which was signed on 3rd March, 1918.

What happened to Trotsky during the leadership struggle?

Stalin *(p.121)* managed to remove Trotsky as a rival during the leadership struggle:

- ☑ Trotsky claimed Stalin *(p.121)* deliberately told him the incorrect date for Lenin's funeral. This meant when Trotsky did not attend, his opponents could claim he did not respect Lenin's legacy.
- ☑ In 1924, Stalin *(p.121)* allied with Zinoviev and Kamenev in supporting the New Economic Policy, in order to oppose Trotsky who wanted rapid industrialisation.
- ☑ Zinoviev and Kamenev worked against Trotsky at the Thirteenth Party Congress in 1924, so that all of Trotsky's ideas were rejected.
- ☑ Trotsky lost his job as Commissar for War in 1925.

What happened to Trotsky during the purges?

During the purges:

- ☑ Trotsky was not in the USSR during the Great Purges of 1936 to 1938 as he lived in exile.
- ☑ Other members of the Communist Party were accused of being 'Trotskyites', a threat to the USSR and communicating with Trotsky in their Show Trials.

How did Trotsky die?

Trotsky was murdered in Mexico on 20th August, 1940 by a member of the NKVD *(p.89)* who forced an ice pick into his head.

Quizzes, amazing exam preparation tools and more at GCSEHistory.com

GENRIKH YAGODA - NKVD

Genrikh Yagoda was the leader of the NKVD when the Great Purge began.

Who was Yagoda?

Genrikh Yagoda joined the Bolshevik *(p.32)* Party in 1907. He was a member of the secret police.

When was Yagoda important?

Yagoda was important between 1934 and 1936.

What role did Yagoda have in the Communist Party?

Yagoda's most important role was as head of the secret police or NKVD *(p.89)* from 1934 to 1936 during the Great Purge.

What happened to Yagoda in the Great Purge?

Yagoda was involved in the Great Purge in 2 ways:

- ☑ He organised and led the initial phase of the Great Purge, including the Trial of the Sixteen in 1936, in which Zinoviev and Kamenev were accused of treason and executed.

- ☑ He was arrested and put on trial in the Trial of the Twenty-One in March 1938. He was found guilty of being a member of a Trotskyite conspiracy and sentenced to death.

When did Yagoda die?

Yagoda was executed by being shot on 13th March, 1938.

NIKOLAI YEZHOV - NKVD

Nikolai Yezhov was the leader of the NKVD when the Great Purge escalated between 1936 and 1938.

Who was Yezhov?

Nikolai Yezhov joined the Communist Party in 1917, was a political commissar in the Red Army during the civil war and replaced Yagoda as the head of the secret police, or NKVD *(p.89)*, in 1936. He was renowned for being vicious and cruel, and he often took part in the torture of the NKVD's victims.

When was Yezhov important?

Yezhov was important during the time of the Great Purge, or Great Terror, between 1936 and 1938.

What was Yezhov's role in the Great Purge?

He was the head of the NKVD *(p.89)* and was responsible for the Great Purge as it escalated and spread to become mass terror. This time period is known as the Yezhovshchina.

Why did Yezhov lose his job?

Stalin *(p.121)* eventually saw Yezhov as suspect and he was arrested and interrogated. He named many of his own family members as suspects which led to hundreds being rounded up and executed.

How did Yezhov die?

He was put on trial, found guilty and executed in February 1940.

DID YOU KNOW?

Yezhov eventually fell from Stalin's favour and was arrested. He confessed to anti-Soviet activity, but later claimed he only did so after being tortured. He was eventually executed in 1940.

GRIGORY ZINOVIEV

Grigory Zinoviev was one of Stalin's opponents in the leadership struggle.

Who was Zinoviev?

Grigory Zinoviev was from a Jewish farming family. He was a member of the Social Democratic Party *(p.32)* and became a member of the Bolshevik *(p.32)* Party when it was created. He spent time in exile with Lenin before returning to Russia in February 1917.

When did Zinoviev join the Communist Party?

Zinoviev joined the Social Democratic Party *(p.32)* in 1901 and became a member of the Bolshevik *(p.32)* Party when it was created in 1903.

What was Lenin's relationship with Zinoviev?

Zinoviev was a close friend of Lenin's, but had opposed Lenin's plan for a revolution in October 1917.

Quizzes, amazing exam preparation tools and more at GCSEHistory.com

What were Zinoviev's political beliefs?

Zinoviev was on the left of the Communist Party. He believed in permanent or world-wide revolution and was against the New Economic Policy, NEP *(p.73)*.

 What did Lenin say about Zinoviev in his 'Testament'?

Lenin criticised Zinoviev for not supporting him in the October Revolution *(p.56)* of 1917 in his 'Testament'.

 What roles did Zinoviev have in the Communist Party?

Zinoviev held 3 key positions of responsibility:

- ☑ In February 1917, Zinoviev was elected chairman of the Council of Commissars of the Petrograd Workers' Commune.
- ☑ In March 1919, he was elected the chairman of the Comintern.
- ☑ From 1921 to 1926, Zinoviev was a full member of the Politburo *(p.71)*.

 What happened to Zinoviev during the leadership struggle with Stalin?

In 1925, Stalin *(p.121)* allied with Kamenev and Zinoviev to defeat Trotsky. Between 1927 and 1929 Stalin turned against Zinoviev and allied with Bukharin.

 What happened to Zinoviev in the Great Purges?

Stalin *(p.121)* viewed Zinoviev as a threat so he was targeted in the Great Purges of 1936 to 1938:

- ☑ He was arrested and put on trial during the Trial of the Sixteen in 1936 with Kamenev.
- ☑ He was accused of the murder of Kirov, plotting to overthrow the government and sabotaging the Five Year Plans.
- ☑ Zinoviev confessed to the crimes of which he was accused to save the lives of his family. He was executed by being shot.

When did Zinoviev die?

Zinoviev was executed after his show trial on 25th August, 1936. He was shot.

DID YOU KNOW?

In 1988, the Soviet government pardoned Zinoviev for the charges that led to his death.

A

Abdicate - to give up a position of power or a responsibility.

Abolish, Abolished - to stop something, or get rid of it.

Abolition - the act of abolishing something, i.e. to stop or get rid of it.

Agricultural - relating to agriculture.

Agriculture - an umbrella term to do with farming, growing crops or raising animals.

Allegiance - loyalty to a person, group or cause.

Alliance - a union between groups or countries that benefits each member.

Allies - parties working together for a common objective, such as countries involved in a war. In both world wars, 'Allies' refers to those countries on the side of Great Britain.

Ambassador - someone, often a diplomat, who represents their state, country or organisation in a different setting or place.

Archaic - to be very old or old-fashioned.

Aristocracy - the highest social class, whose members gain their power from possessing land, property and money.

Aristocrat - a person who belongs to the aristocracy.

Artillery - large guns used in warfare.

Assassinate - to murder someone, usually an important figure, often for religious or political reasons.

Assassination - the act of murdering someone, usually an important person.

Assembly - a meeting of a group of people, often as part of a country's government, to make decisions.

Autocracy - a system of government where the ruler has absolute power over their country.

Autocrat - a ruler who has absolute power over their country.

Autonomy - independence or self-government.

B

Bolshevik, Bolsheviks - was a Russian radical Marxist revolutionary group, founded by Vladimir Lenin and Alexander Bogdanov in 1903. A Bolshevik is someone who is a member of that party.

Bourgeoisie - the capitalists who owned the means of production, i.e. land, banks and factories, in Marxist ideology.

Boycott - a way of protesting or bringing about change by refusing to buy something or use services.

Bribe, Bribery, Bribes - to dishonestly persuade someone to do something for you in return for money or other inducements.

C

Cabinet - politically, the group of senior ministers responsible for controlling government policy.

Campaign - a political movement to get something changed; in military terms, it refers to a series of operations to achieve a goal.

Capitalism - the idea of goods and services being exchanged for money, private ownership of property and businesses, and acceptance of a hierarchical society.

Ceasefire - when the various sides involved in conflict agree to stop fighting.

Censorship - the control of information in the media by a government, whereby information considered obscene or unacceptable is suppressed.

Civil rights - the rights a citizen has to political or social freedoms such as the right to vote or freedom of speech.

Civilian - a non-military person.

Claim - someone's assertion of their right to something - for example, a claim to the throne.

Clergy - those ordained for religious duties, especially in the Christian Church.

Communal - referring to something that is shared by all members of a community, be it an action or possession etc.

Commune - a place where a group of people live and work together and share resources.

Communism - the belief, based on the ideas of Karl Marx, that all people should be equal in society without government, money or private property. Everything is owned by by the people, and each person receives according to need.

Communist - a believer in communism.

Conference - a formal meeting to discuss common issues of interest or concern.

Conscription - mandatory enlistment of people into a state service, usually the military.

Conservative - someone who dislikes change and prefers traditional values. It can also refer to a member of the Conservative Party.

Consolidate - to strengthen a position, often politically, by bringing several things together into a more effective whole.

Constitution - rules, laws or principles that set out how a country is governed.

Constitutional - relating to the constitution.

Constitutional monarchy - political system in which a monarch's powers and authority are limited by a constitution.

Consumer goods - products that people buy.

Cooperate, Cooperation - to work together to achieve a common aim. Frequently used in relation to politics, economics or law.

Corrupt - when someone is willing to act dishonestly for their own personal gain.

Coup - a sudden, violent and illegal overthrow of the government by a small group - for example, the chiefs of an army.

Culture - the ideas, customs, and social behaviour of a particular people or society.

Currency - an umbrella term for any form of legal tender, but most commonly referring to money.

D

Debt - when something, usually money, is owed by a person, organisation or institution to another.

Decree - an official order with the force of law behind it.

Democracy - a political system where a population votes for its government on a regular basis. The word is Greek for 'the rule of people' or 'people power'.

Democratic - relating to or supporting the principles of democracy.

Deport - to expel someone from a country and, usually, return them to their homeland.

Deportation - the act of deporting someone.

Deterrent - something that discourages an action or behaviour.

Dictator - a ruler with absolute power over a country, often acquired by force.

Dictatorship - a form of government where an individual or small group has total power, ruling without tolerance for other views or opposition.

Dictatorship of the Proletariat - the belief that, whilst the proletariat would eventually come to rule itself as proposed by Karl Marx, for now they were not ready, and required a 'dictator' to guide them until they were able to rule themselves.

Discriminate, Discrimination - to treat a person or group of people differently and in an unfair way.

Dispute - a disagreement or argument; often used to describe conflict between different countries.

Dissolution, Dissolve - the formal ending of a partnership, organisation or official body.

Divine right - the belief held by monarchs or rulers that they are given the right to rule by God.

E

Economic - relating to the economy; also used when justifying something in terms of profitability.

Economy - a country, state or region's position in terms of production and consumption of goods and services, and the supply of money.

Empire - a group of states or countries ruled over and controlled by a single monarch.

Estate, Estates - an extensive area of land, usually in the country and including a large house. It tends to be owned by one person, family or organisation.

Exile - to be banned from one's original country, usually as a punishment or for political reasons.

Export - to transport goods for sale to another country.

Extreme - furthest from the centre or any given point. If someone holds extreme views, they are not moderate and are considered radical.

F

Famine - a severe food shortage resulting in starvation and death, usually the result of bad harvests.

Foreign policy - a government's strategy for dealing with other nations.

Free elections - elections in which voters are free to vote without interference.

Front - in war, the area where fighting is taking place.

Full employment - when virtually everyone able and willing to work in a country has a job.

G

General strike - occurs when many different groups of workers strike at the same time, often with the aim of bringing a country to a standstill.

Gulag - a forced labour camp in the USSR.

H

Haemophilia - a genetic blood disorder where the blood does not clot properly.

Harvest - the process of gathering and collecting crops.

Heavy industry - the manufacture of large and/or heavy items in bulk, or industries which involve large and heavy equipment and/or facilities. Examples are the iron, coal, steel and electricity industries.

Hierarchies, Hierarchy - the ranking of people according to authority, for example a colonel in the army being higher than a corporal.

I

Ideology - a set of ideas and ideals, particularly around political ideas or economic policy, often shared by a group of people.

Illiterate - unable to read or write.

Import - to bring goods or services into a different country to sell.

Independence, Independent - to be free of control, often meaning by another country, allowing the people of a nation the ability to govern themselves.

Indoctrinate, Indoctrination - to teach someone to accept a set of beliefs without reservation or question.

Industrial - related to industry, manufacturing and/or production.

Industrialisation, Industrialise, Industrialised - the process of developing industry in a country or region where previously there was little or none.

Industry - the part of the economy concerned with turning raw materials into into manufactured goods, for example making furniture from wood.

Inferior - lower in rank, status or quality.

Inflation - the general increase in the prices of goods which means money does not buy as much as it used to.

Informant - someone who passes important information to another person or organisation, such as the police.

Infrastructure - the basic physical and organisational facilities a society or country needs to function, such as transport networks, communications and power.

International relations - the relationships between different countries.

K

Kulak - a richer peasant who had sufficient money to own land or a farm.

L

Left wing - used to describe political groups or individuals with beliefs that are usually centered around socialism and the idea of reform.

Legislation - a term for laws when they are considered collectively, for example housing legislation.

Legitimacy, Legitimate - accepted by law or conforming to the rules; can be defended as valid.

Liberal - politically, someone who believes in allowing personal freedom without too much control by the government or state.

Literate - someone who can read and write.

M

Manifesto - the stated policies or aims of a political party or person, normally published before an election.

Massacre - the deliberate and brutal slaughter of many people.

Means of production - resources which enable the production of goods, such as tools, factories and raw materials.

Merchant, Merchants - someone who sells goods or services.

Middle class - refers to the socio-economic group which includes people who are educated and have professional jobs, such as teachers or lawyers.

Military force - the use of armed forces.

Militia - an army created from the general population.

Minister - a senior member of government, usually responsible for a particular area such as education or finance.

Mir - was a village in which the community holds the land jointly but farms it individually in tsarist Russia.

Mobilisation - the action of a country getting ready for war by preparing and organising its armed forces.

Moderate - someone who is not extreme.

Modernise - to update something to make it suitable for modern times, often by using modern equipment or modern ideas.

Monarchists - people in favour of living in a country governed by a monarchy.

Monarchy - a form of government in which the head of state is a monarch, a king or queen.

Morale - general mood of a group of people.

Mutiny - a rebellion or revolt, in particular by soldiers or sailors against their commanding officers.

Mystical - relating to magical, religious or spiritual powers.

N

Nationalism, Nationalist, Nationalistic - identifying with your own nation and supporting its interests, often to the detriment or exclusion of other nations.

Nobility - the social class ranked directly below royalty.

Noble, Nobles - another word for aristocrat - a member of the highest and richest class in society.

O

Oath - a solemn promise with special significance, often relating to future behaviour or actions.

Occupation - the action, state or period when somewhere is taken over and occupied by a military force.

P

POW, Prisoner of war, Prisoners of war - somebody who has been captured and taken prisoner by enemy forces.

Parliament - a group of politicians who make the laws of their country, usually elected by the population.

Patriotic - a strong love of and support for one's country.

Peasant - a poor farmer.

Persecute - to treat someone unfairly because of their race, religion or political beliefs.

Persecution - hostility towards or harassment of someone, usually due to their race, religion or political beliefs.

Pilgrimage - journey undertaken to a sacred place, usually for religious or spiritual reasons.

Police state - a totalitarian country in which the police have a great deal of power to control the people and suppress opposition.

Population - the number of people who live in a specified place.

Poverty - the state of being extremely poor.

Pragmatic - taking a practical approach; being sensible and realistic.

President - the elected head of state of a republic.

Prevent, Preventative, Preventive - steps taken to stop something from happening.

Printing press - a machine that reproduces writing and images by using ink on paper, making many identical copies.

Production - a term used to describe how much of something is made, for example saying a factory has a high production rate.

Profit - generally refers to financial gain; the amount of money made after deducting buying, operating or production costs.

Propaganda - biased information aimed at persuading people to think a certain way.

Prosecute - to institute or conduct legal proceedings against a person or organisation.

Prosperity - the state of thriving, enjoying good fortune and/or social status.

Province, Provinces - part of an empire or a country denoting areas that have been divided for administrative purposes.

R

Radical, Radicalism - people who want complete or extensive change, usually politically or socially.

Rationing - limiting goods that are in high demand and short supply.

Real wages - a person's income in terms of how much they can buy after taking inflation into account.

Rebellion - armed resistance against a government or leader, or resistance to other authority or control.

Rebels - people who rise in opposition or armed resistance against an established government or leader.

Reform, Reforming - change, usually in order to improve an institution or practice.

Regent - the person who rules when the king is away, incapacitated or too young to rule.

Reign - a period of power, usually by a monarch.

Relief - something that reduces pressure on people, often through financial or practical support.

Reparations - payments made by the defeated countries in a war to the victors to help pay for the cost of and damage from the fighting.

Repress, Repression - politically, to prevent something or control people by by force.

Repressive - a harsh or authoritarian action; usually used to describe governmental abuse of power.

Republic - a state or country run by elected representatives and an elected/nominated president. There is no monarch.

Requisition - to take something, usually by official order, such as a government taking food from peasants.

Revolution - the forced overthrow of a government or social system by its own people.

Right wing - a political view with beliefs centred around nationalism and a desire for an authoritarian government opposed to communism.

Riots - violent disturbances involving a crowd of people.

Russification - a policy implemented by the tsars in Russia to enforce Russian culture and language on non-Russian ethnic groups.

S

Sabotage - to deliberately destroy, damage or obstruct, especially to gain a political or military advantage.

Sanitation - conditions relating to public health, such as the sewage system and drinking water supply.

Self-determination, Self-determined - in politics, the process where a nation decides its own statehood and whether it will rule itself rather than be part of a larger empire.

Serfdom - the condition or state of being a serf.

Socialism - a political and economic system where most resources, such as factories and businesses, are owned by the state or workers with the aim of achieving greater equality between rich and poor.

Socialist - one who believes in the principles of socialism.

Soviet - an elected workers' council at local, regional or national level in the former Soviet Union. It can also be a reference to the Soviet Union or the USSR.

Standard of living - level of wealth and goods available to an individual or group.

State, States - an area of land or a territory ruled by one government.

Strategy - a plan of action outlining how a goal will be achieved.

Strike - a refusal by employees to work as a form of protest, usually to bring about change in their working conditions. It puts pressure on their employer, who cannot run the business without workers.

Subsistence, Subsistence farming, Subsistent - a type of farming in which farmers only grow or produce enough for their own use, with no surplus to sell.

Successor - someone who succeeds the previous person, such as a leader who takes over the role from the previous holder.

Suppress, Suppression - the use of force to stop something, such as a protest.

T

Tactic - a strategy or method of achieving a goal.

Territories, Territory - an area of land under the control of a ruler/country.

Trade unions - organised groups of workers who cooperate to make their lives better at work. For example, they might negotiate for better pay and then organise a strike if one is refused.

Treason - the crime of betraying one's country, often involving an attempt to overthrow the government or kill the monarch.

Treaty - a formal agreement, signed and ratified by two or more parties.

Tsar - the Russian word for emperor; can also be spelled 'czar'.

U

Ultimatum - a final demand, with the threat of consequences if it is not met.

Upper class - a socio-economic group consisting of the richest people in a society who are wealthy because they own land or property.

V

Veto - the right to reject a decision or proposal.

W

Welfare - wellbeing; often refers to money and services given to the poorest people.

Working class - socio-economic group consisting of those engaged in waged labour, especially manual work or industry, who typically do not have much money.

Z

Zemstvos - elected local assemblies, set up Russia in 1864 to administer local affairs.

Lightning Source UK Ltd.
Milton Keynes UK
HW052311231020
132UK00003B/45